FACTOLOGY
BUGS

Open up a world of information!

ARE YOU READY TO EXPLORE...

Ready to go beneath the surface of the bug world, Factologists? There are an estimated 1.4 BILLION insects for every human on Earth, but there's still so much we don't know about these astonishing creepy-crawlies. Since humans first walked upright, bugs, insects and minibeasts have influenced and inspired us... and even kept us well fed.

It's time to investigate the inside-out world of invertebrates! Get to grips with the mechanics of bug bodies, learn about ancient giants, encounter Earth's strangest faces and build a beetle hotel! From the tiniest tick to the biggest tarantula, you're about to inspect all manner of insects. Let's find out why there's so much buzz about these bugs...

CHAPTER 1

THE WONDERFUL WORLD OF BUGS

Some bugs are beautiful, others are annoying and lots are really gross, but all of them are important. Like an invisible force, they keep much of our world working and without them, life would be completely different...

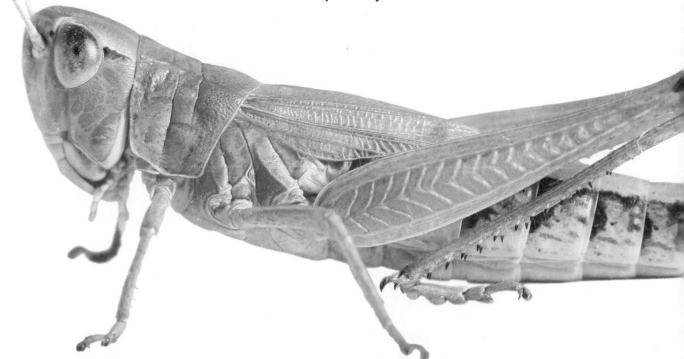

IT'S A BUG'S LIFE

Insects have been around for over 470 million years – since before dinosaurs! – and these days over a million different species have been discovered. In fact, it's thought that 90% of all animal species on Earth are insects! Bugs come in all shapes and sizes and scientists have organised them into 29 different categories (called orders) based on their features. Let's check out some of the groups they belong to...

BEETLES

There are more than 370,000 known species of beetle in the world. This brilliant bug belongs to the insect order Coleoptera, which means sheath-winged. Beetles are found all over the world on land and in fresh water. They generally use their hind wings for flying – the front pair are hard wing cases called elytra, which cover and protect the flight wings when they're not in use.

FACT MORE THAN A THIRD OF ALL EARTH'S INSECT SPECIES ARE BEETLES!

▲ Be on the lookout for the harmless wasp beetle from May to August

This five-horned rhinoceros beetle is ready for take off!

BEES, WASPS AND ANTS

These insects are one of the largest groups. Some people don't realise they're in the same order, called Hymenoptera, but almost all of these creepy-crawlies have similar segmented bodies with a narrow waist. Ants live in organised colonies, with a queen and lots of female workers, and so do some kinds of bees and wasps. However, many species of wasps and bees also live on their own.

Bees and wasps are important pollinators, moving pollen between flowering plants

These southern wood ants defend themselves by spraying acid!

Assassin bugs impale their victims with their beak, suck the fluid from them and use their body as camouflage!

TRUE BUGS

To entomologists, true bugs are a particular group of insects. They belong to the Hemiptera order and over 85,000 species have been discovered. This group of truly remarkable insects all have piercing, sucking mouthparts that they use to feed. True bugs also often have large antennae divided into segments, soft bodies and two pairs of wings.

FACT SCIENTISTS WHO STUDY BUGS ARE CALLED ENTOMOLOGISTS.

The Goliath birdwing butterfly is one of the largest species in the world

Moths are often dull-coloured to keep them camouflaged but this rosy maple moth definitely stands out!

FACT OVER ONE MILLION INSECT SPECIES HAVE BEEN NAMED AND IT'S THOUGHT FOUR MILLION MORE ARE STILL UNCATEGORISED!

BUTTERFLIES AND MOTHS

One of the largest groups of insects, butterflies and moths belongs to the insect order of Lepidoptera. These insects spend most of their lives as caterpillars before going through an amazing transformation. Butterflies and moths look similar but there are differences. Butterflies are usually more colourful and have different antennae – moths' antennae are plain or feathery, while butterflies' are more club-shaped. Moths are active at night (nocturnal) and butterflies are awake during the day (diurnal).

HALTERE

▲ Thanks to their balancing rods, true flies like this crane fly are super-acrobatic flyers!

TRUE FLIES

More than 110,000 species of true flies have been discovered. These interesting insects belong to the order Diptera. True flies only have one set of wings. Instead of rear wings they have two short balancing rods, called halteres, which help steady the insects during flight.

Horseflies even annoyed the Ancient Greeks – the great thinker Aeschylus blamed them for making people mad!

FACT THERE ARE APPROXIMATELY 1.4 BILLION INSECTS FOR EVERY ONE PERSON.

◀ Grasshoppers have ears on their knees! This clever design helps them hear the songs of other grasshoppers

A grasshopper emerging from its shed skin – most need to moult five times

GRASSHOPPERS AND CRICKETS

Famous for being noisy, grasshoppers, crickets and their relatives belong to the order Orthoptera, which has over 24,000 species. These insects are awesome jumpers thanks to their long, powerful legs. Most of this group communicate by chirping, known as their song. Grasshoppers chirp by rubbing their legs over their wings and crickets sing by rubbing their wings together. These magnificent beasts make music!

BUG BODIES

Today's bugs have evolved from ancient arthropods – early animals that first developed more than 500 million years ago. Arthropods have a hard outer skeleton (called an exoskeleton) that supports and protects their bodies. This group of creatures includes all kinds of brilliant bugs, with insects being the biggest arthropod group by far. Read on to find out what makes an insect an insect

EXOSKELETON

Insects have exoskeletons made of a hard material called chitin. Because their exoskeletons are stiff and can't bend, they have joints (bendable sections) that allow them to move. As insects grow, they become too big for their exoskeleton. When this happens, they shed the ill-fitting outer layer and replace it with a new one, in a process called moulting.

FACT THE SCIENTIFIC WORD EXOSKELETON MEANS OUTSIDE SKELETON.

HEAD
THORAX
ABDOMEN

BODY

All insects have bodies that are divided into three sections – a head, thorax (the middle part), and abdomen (the end part). The head is home to the insect's sensory apparatus – its mouth, antennae and eyes. The thorax contains its digestive organs and the abdomen is where the creepy-crawly's reproductive organs are.

◀ The abdomen houses important organs like the heart and part of the insect's digestive system

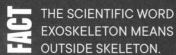
This rose chafer has a beautiful shiny green exoskeleton

ANTENNA

A lot of insects have two long sense organs, called antenna, near the front of their head. These clever feelers allow the insect to understand its surroundings, helping it touch, taste, hear and smell. The world's very different to bugs – and how they sense it needs to be too!

▶ A cockchafer beetle using its antenna to check the direction of the wind!

LEGS

Insects have three pairs of jointed legs that are attached to their thorax. Most species mainly use their legs for walking, but a lot of insects also use their forelegs to savagely attack prey!

This praying mantis is ready to fight!

EYES

Most insects have a pair of eyes that can see in almost every direction. Known as compound eyes, these peepers put ours to shame – they hold thousands of tiny lenses, which are able to pick up lots of images all at the same time. This helps the clever critters detect movement from different angles all at once, giving them super-speedy reflexes!

STINGER

Some insects – such as bees, wasps, hornets and ants – have stingers at their tail end, which they use to defend themselves. If the insect feels threatened, its stinger releases venom, which it injects into the victim's skin. Ouch!

▶ Watch out for this wasp's sharp stinger!

FACT SOME INSECTS ONLY GROW WINGS WHEN THEY'RE LOOKING FOR MATES. QUEEN ANTS CHEW OFF THEIR WINGS WHEN THEY'RE READY TO LAY EGGS!

MOUTHPARTS

Insects eat in different ways. Some creepy-crawlies – such as mosquitoes, fleas and lice – use a thin tube called a proboscis to puncture tissue and suck up liquid food. Other insects – including butterflies, moths and bees – have a proboscis that's only used when their feet touch something tasty. Insects such as grasshoppers, beetles and caterpillars nibble, chew and grind their food with jaws that move from side to side.

A monarch butterfly caterpillar munching on a milkweed plant leaf

WINGS

Flying insects usually have two pairs of wings that are see-through and thin. The wings are formed from their exoskeleton and are tougher than they look!

Some insects have hard wing cases, known as elytra. These wings look like a shell and hide a second, softer set of hind wings. The elytra help the insect take off, then the softer wings beat to push it forwards and steer. For these arthropods, flying isn't as hard as it looks!

▼ A rosemary beetle with wide open elytra prepares for lift off!

Tiny hairs on the green lacewing's wings stop spiders' webs from sticking to them

NATURE'S GARDENERS

Creepy-crawlies are natural gardeners! They play an important role in the life cycle of plants and help keep crops and plant life healthy too. From pollination and treating soil to helping dead things break down, insects are an essential part of our ecosystems!

Action stations

Insects help flowers and trees reproduce with a process called pollination. Hoverflies, bumblebees, honeybees and butterflies all feed on the sweet sugary fluid found inside flowering plants – it's called nectar. As they enjoy this sweet treat, pollen from the flower sticks to them. So when they fly to a new flower to carry on feeding, the insects transfer pollen. This fertilises the flower and allows it to produce healthy seeds that'll grow into new plants. Insects are the most common pollinators in nature, but plants are also pollinated by birds, bats and even the wind!

SOIL STARS

Whether it's on farms, in gardens or part of the countryside, soil is everywhere – and insects are a vital part of keeping it healthy. Bugs help soil in a number of ways

✱ Soil aeration
Insect activity helps air enter into the soil, which lets stale carbon dioxide out and makes room for fresh new oxygen. This creates fertile soil that drains well and even helps plants thrive and absorb water.

✱ Burrowers
Bugs that burrow into soil, such as ants and beetles, help distribute water with the channels they create. They make tiny water tunnels!

✱ Fertilisation
Insect poo, also known as frass, provides nutrients and helps fertilise soil.

BRAND-NEW SPECIES HAVE EVEN BEEN FOUND IN FRASS!

Flower power

Around 75% of all flowering plants need pollinators (animals that help with pollination) to pass pollen from plant to plant, and plants have developed clever ways of luring them in!

Colourful flowers do a great job of attracting pollinators to plants. It's thought bees are more attracted to bright blue and violet flowers, butterflies prefer yellow, orange and pink flowers and beetles like white or cream colours.

Releasing nice smells is another way plants draw pollinators to them. When it comes to scent, beetles are more attracted to musty or spicy pongs and bees and butterflies prefer lavender, mint and herby scents! Pores in their antennae work like a nose!

FAST⚡FACT

Bumblebees are 'buzz pollinators' – they grab flowers and vibrate their flight muscles to loosen pollen!

Breaking it down

Another important way insects help soil is as decomposers. Also known as detritivores, these are scavenger bugs who feed on decomposing matter. There are three main groups of detritivore insects: ones that munch on dead or dying plants, others that eat dead animals and ones that feed on animal poo. These hungry scavengers help recycle nutrients back into the soil and create top soil, the nutrient-rich layer that helps plants grow. Scavenger bugs include beetles, blow flies, termites, flies and cockroaches.

FAST⚡FACT

Detritivores are also sometimes known as saprophages. This name comes from the Greek words saprós, meaning rotten, and phagein, meaning eat.

A downy emerald dragonfly hatching sequence, from left to right clockwise

HERE WE GROW

They may look different but all insects grow in a similar way. Read on to discover how these awesome critters develop...

Insect life cycles

An animal's life cycle is the series of changes it goes through during its life – for insects, this involves three or four stages. Understanding the cycle is important as it allows entomologists (scientists who study insects) to work out whether a bug will be a pest or beneficial to its surroundings – and how to attract them or manage their numbers around crops.

Magical metamorphosis

When insects grow and develop, the process is called metamorphosis (which means 'to change form'). This refers to the different stages the insects go through as they grow from an egg into an adult.

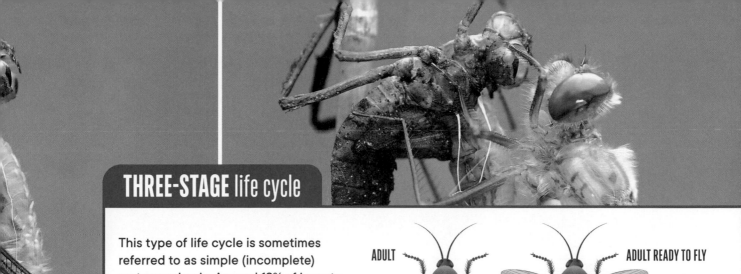

THREE-STAGE life cycle

This type of life cycle is sometimes referred to as simple (incomplete) metamorphosis. Around 12% of insects grow like this. Insects that go through simple metamorphosis have three life stages – egg, nymph and adult. Eggs are laid and then, once the insects have hatched, they grow and become adults. Young insects are known as nymphs and with this life cycle nymphs look like mini-adults!

With the three-stage life cycle, an insect's wings start developing as buds on its thorax during its later nymph stages. The wings continue to grow until the bug is an adult. Some species of insect that experience a three-stage life cycle include dragonflies, grasshoppers, earwigs and cockroaches.

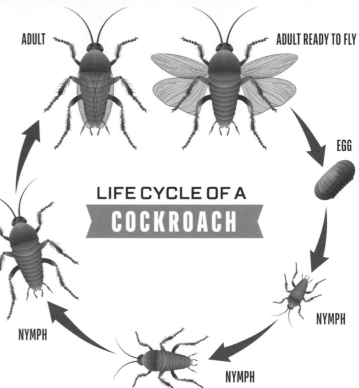

ADULT

ADULT READY TO FLY

EGG

LIFE CYCLE OF A
COCKROACH

NYMPH

NYMPH

NYMPH

◄ The fully formed dragonfly has finally finished hunting and it's ready for a feast! Dragonflies can live for up to eight weeks and spend much of that time hunting smaller flying insects

FAST⚡FACT

Froghopper nymphs protect themselves from predators by creating white foamy bubbles to hide in. The clever creatures create the foam – which is known as cuckoo spit – by squeezing plant sap out of their bum!

ALL CHANGE!

Check out these amazing insect transformations!

EGG

CATERPILLAR
(LARVA)

CHRYSALIS
(PUPA)

1 When monarch butterflies hatch from their eggs, they become stripy caterpillars. They shed their skin five times in this larval stage, and then form a chrysalis. After 10 to 14 days, a beautiful orange, black and white butterfly emerges ready to fly!

2 When ladybird larvae hatch, they're spiky, black and worm-like. They grow from a blob-like yellow or orange pupa and finally emerge from their pupal case as a cute red bug with black dots!

3 Hickory horned devil caterpillars are blue-green, orange or brown and have several pairs of long, curved, black-tipped orange horns on their back. These 15cm-long larvae burrow into the ground and transform into large, orange and yellow royal walnut moths!

EGG

LARVAE

LARVAE

ADULT

PUPA

LARVAE

FOUR-STAGE life cycle

This life cycle is also known as complete metamorphosis. Insects that go through this life cycle have four stages of growth: egg, larva, pupa and adult. With complete metamorphosis, larvae look very different to the adult insects – much more than us humans!

The four-stage life cycle begins when the female insect lays her eggs. Then the larvae hatch and grow bigger. During this stage, the insect sheds and replaces its skin several times in a process called moulting. The next part of the metamorphosis is the pupa stage. This is when the larva rests and transforms into an adult. The insect creates a protective case (moths spin a silk cocoon that covers them, for example) where the larva's body is broken down and rebuilt – this is why the adult insect looks so different. After a final moult, the adult insect emerges, fully transformed!

With this life cycle, if an insect has wings, they develop internally during the pupa stage. Insects that go through complete metamorphosis include beetles, butterflies, moths, wasps and bees.

ADULT
MONARCH
BUTTERFLY

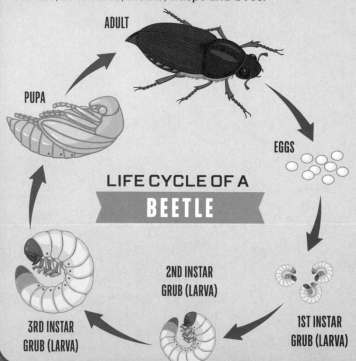

ADULT

PUPA

EGGS

LIFE CYCLE OF A
BEETLE

2ND INSTAR
GRUB (LARVA)

3RD INSTAR
GRUB (LARVA)

1ST INSTAR
GRUB (LARVA)

NORTH AMERICA

With grasslands, forests, deserts and mountains, North America has a wide variety of bug life. The periodical cicada spends 99.5% of its life underground. After around 15 years, up to 1.5 million cicadas emerge at the same time and 'sing' loudly to attract a mate (which sounds a bit like a buzzing maraca!).

A beautiful newly emerged cicada

MAKE YOURSELF

At Home!

Bugs account for 90% of life forms on the planet and they're the world's most diverse group of organisms. No matter where you travel, bugs are part of the ecosystem and they can be found on every continent!

ASIA

Asia is home to bugs of all shapes and sizes – including one of the world's longest insects. Found in the rainforests of Borneo, the Pharnacia kirby stick insect can grow up to 50cm in length!

The brilliant Asian lady beetle measures just 0.7cm long and has been introduced to other countries to protect crops from aphids

OCEANIA

Oceania has some of the world's most amazing bugs. Insects found on this continent include spiders, stick insects, centipedes and ants. It's home to the giant centipede, which measures up to 15cm long! At 1.5cm long, termites are much smaller, but create massive mounds above and below the ground, which usually reach up to 5m high!

Termite colonies have a million members and live in mounds like this

A giant centipede

AFRICA

Being the world's hottest continent makes Africa a challenging place for bugs to live. Over half the land there is dry or desert and insects must survive in high temperatures with little food or water. Found in East Africa, the devil's flower mantis is one of the largest species of praying mantis in the world. This sneaky critter uses camouflage to hide from prey, mimicking leaves until a tasty snack flies by!

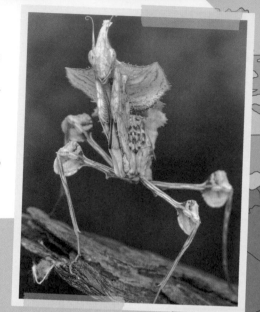

Locusts eat their own body weight in food every day! Swarms of up to one billion bugs can be seen in the African sky looking for crops to eat!

ECUADOR

The magnificent blue morpho butterfly lives in the rainforests of Ecuador

AMAZON RAINFOREST

BRAZIL

South American country Brazil has the world's biggest range of insects – there are over 90,000 different species there!

SOUTH AMERICA

Stretching across nine countries, the Amazon is Earth's largest rainforest and home to more than 2.5 million species of insect. Leaf-cutter ants, rhinoceros beetles, cockroaches and termites are among the amazing bugs that can be found there.

Some Rhino beetles can live for up to three years

It's thought that ants can hold up to 50x their bodyweight. Superheroes!

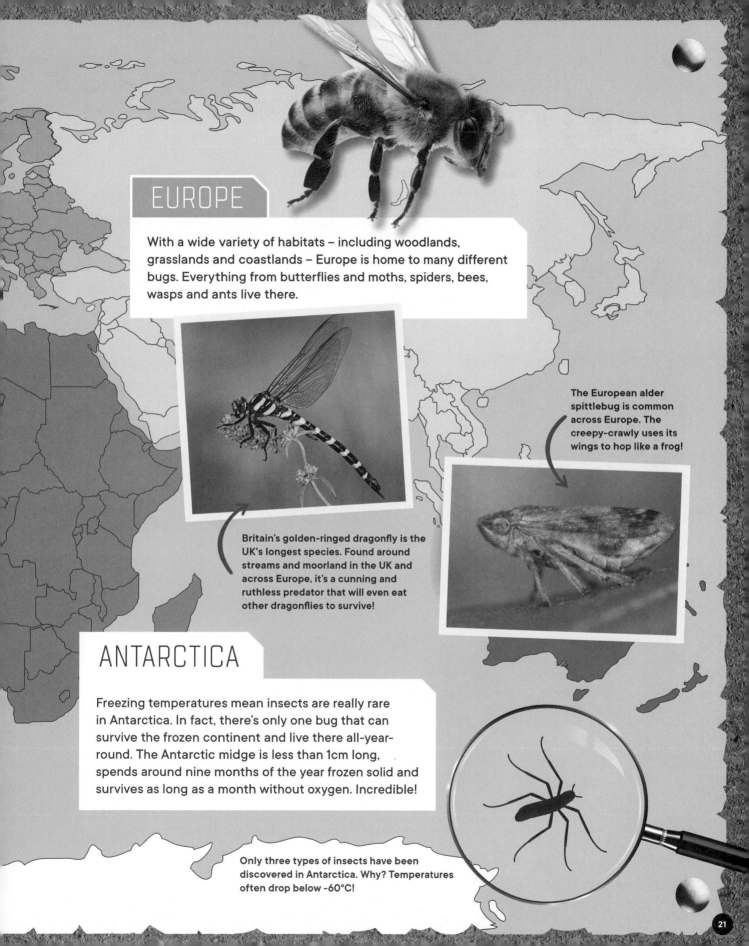

EUROPE

With a wide variety of habitats – including woodlands, grasslands and coastlands – Europe is home to many different bugs. Everything from butterflies and moths, spiders, bees, wasps and ants live there.

The European alder spittlebug is common across Europe. The creepy-crawly uses its wings to hop like a frog!

Britain's golden-ringed dragonfly is the UK's longest species. Found around streams and moorland in the UK and across Europe, it's a cunning and ruthless predator that will even eat other dragonflies to survive!

ANTARCTICA

Freezing temperatures mean insects are really rare in Antarctica. In fact, there's only one bug that can survive the frozen continent and live there all-year-round. The Antarctic midge is less than 1cm long, spends around nine months of the year frozen solid and survives as long as a month without oxygen. Incredible!

Only three types of insects have been discovered in Antarctica. Why? Temperatures often drop below -60°C!

BUG ATTACK!

With so many predators looking for a tasty insect snack, bugs need to work hard to survive! Their small size makes them vulnerable but they've developed lots of weird and wonderful ways to protect themselves from the hungry creatures that see them as food

25221. Neg Em 34455

Hair raising

Some tarantulas put off predators in the same way a porcupine uses its quills to defend itself. When the tarantula feels threatened, the clever crawler takes aim and vibrates its back legs to fling clouds of tiny bristles known as urticating hairs from its abdomen at their potential attacker. The small, irritating hairs lodge in the predator's eyes, nose or mouth and the spider can make its escape while its pursuer is being distracted.

Colour camouflage

Many insects are masters of disguise, using camouflage so well they can hide in plain sight without worrying about being spotted!

When the golden tortoise beetle is under threat, it changes colour to make predators think it's a poisonous insect. The beetle usually looks metallic-gold thanks to pockets of fluid in the layers of its outer shell that reflect light. But if it's disturbed, the reflective fluid dries up and its colour changes to dark red – in under two minutes!

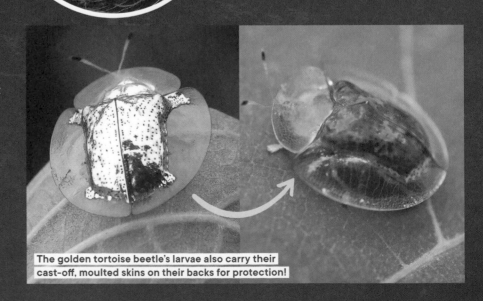

The golden tortoise beetle's larvae also carry their cast-off, moulted skins on their backs for protection!

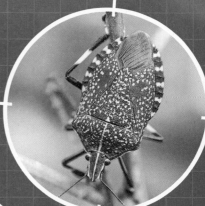

Crushing it

Some insects rely on their super-tough exoskeleton to avoid being eaten. The diabolical ironclad beetle's body is basically crush-proof! Seriously, it's like a tiny tank. It's no wonder we're looking to the insect world to improve our own materials – Phloeodes diabolicus has a rugged exoskeleton so strong, it can survive getting run over by a car!

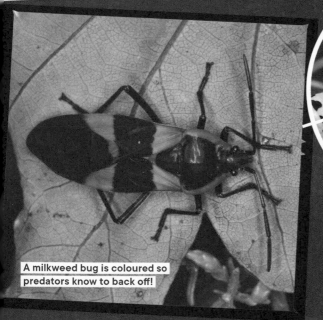

A milkweed bug is coloured so predators know to back off!

Bad taste

Some insects use colour to let predators know they're not going to be a tasty treat. This is known as aposematic colouration. Bugs are usually brightly coloured to show the world they'll taste bad – and might even be poisonous – if they're eaten. Colour combinations such as red and black (ladybirds and milkweed bugs), orange and black (boxelder bugs and monarch butterflies), and yellow and black (bees and wasps) are often used to put predators off.

SMELLY DEFENCE

Many insects use smelly odours to protect themselves! Check out our top four stinkers

1 Whenever a shield beetle feels threatened, it releases a yucky foul-smelling liquid from its abdomen.

2 If touched, some swallowtail caterpillars wave a Y-shaped gland in the air to release a toxic whiff!

3 Sawfly larvae emit a combination of rancid chemicals. Oh, what a pong!

4 When darkling beetles are disturbed they poke their tails in the air. If it continues, they expel a dark, pongy fluid!

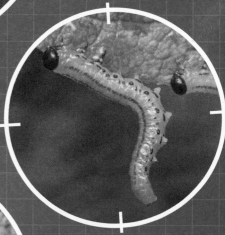

CAN YOU SPOT

...THE DARK CRIMSON UNDERWING MOTHS HIDING ON THIS TREE BARK? Their patterned wings provide excellent camouflage from predators, helping them blend in with their environment.

Spray it again!

Some insects stay safe by spraying nasty substances at predators to distract them. This clever technique makes the attacker stop to clean itself and gives the insect enough time to escape.

Bombardier beetles deter would-be attackers by blasting a jet of hot, toxic chemicals at them! The beetle creates the powerful substance by mixing two chemicals usually stored separately in its body. Then, when a predator – such as an ant, frog or lizard – attacks, it sprays the nasty mixture from its bum!

Leg it!

Some insects – such as craneflies and grasshoppers – have special built-in fracture lines at joints in their legs. This allows the bug's leg to break off cleanly if a predator grips it, leaving the insect to escape. If the leg is lost when the insect is young, it may even grow back!

AMAZING MIMICS

Warning off predators with bright colours works so well that some insects disguise themselves as insects that predators know to avoid. Other insects mimic plants to avoid being eaten! Check out these masters of disguise...

1 Looking like a large bumblebee helps the clear-winged sphinx moth stay safe. It even visits flowers during the day to complete its disguise – that's dedication!

2 Wasp beetles use wasp-like colours and patterns to ward off hungry birds. They also make a distinct wasp-like buzzing sound when they feel threatened!

3 It's thought that stick insects began imitating plants as early as 126 million years ago. Peckish predators can't spot them!

4 Dead leaf mantises are amazingly good at imitating dead, broken and decaying leaves. These sneaky critters even sway like a leaf if they're bothered!

WATER WONDERS

Insects that live in or on water have cleverly adapted to their environment and have special features that help them thrive in their watery habitat. Time to dive in and find out more about water insects

AMBUSH ACTION →

WHERE? Common across the UK. Water scorpions are vicious ambush predators! These sneaky insects hide underwater among aquatic plants, using a snorkel-like tube to breathe that sticks out from their back end. When unsuspecting prey comes along, the scorpion-like water bugs attack! Eating bugs, minnows, tadpoles and worms, they use their long front legs to seize prey. They're aquatic attackers!

FACT THIS DARK BROWN DIVER HAS A FLAT, LEAF-SHAPED BODY AND A LONG TAIL. IF YOU SEE ONE, DON'T BE ALARMED – THEY'RE NOT ACTUALLY SCORPIONS!

The underside of a water scavenger beetle, caught in action mid-swim!

← UNDERWATER MOVERS

WHERE? Marshy freshwater lakes across the UK. Water scavenger beetles have a rare way of moving around underwater – they scurry about upside down just beneath the surface! These balletic beetles use their heads to hang from the water's surface and move their legs to swim, just like they're walking on the underside of a glass table!

It's thought the beetles breathe underwater using tiny hairs on their abdomen and legs to trap air bubbles. This also helps pin the beetles to the underside of the water. Scientists think the aquatic acrobats move about underwater to steer clear of predators!

AMAZING MAYFLIES

WHERE? Freshwater wetlands. Water-loving mayflies begin life as eggs on a riverbed before hatching and becoming nymphs. Most of a mayfly's life is spent in the water as the young insects feed on algae and other plants and then develop into adults.

Mayflies are the only insects that moult – shed their other layer of skin – after they've developed working wings. Once they're grown, the insects emerge from the water and fly somewhere sheltered on the riverbank. Then they moult to reveal shiny new skin and wings, before heading back to the water to mate. It takes mayflies around two years to become fully grown but the adult stage of their lives usually only lasts for a few hours. So short!

FACT ADULT MAYFLIES DON'T EAT – THEY DO ALL THEIR FEEDING WHEN THEY'RE NYMPHS.

← SKATE STARS

WHERE? Calm or slow-moving water. Also known as water striders, pond skaters can walk on water! These incredible insects are able to do this thanks to three pairs of long legs and special feet. Tiny hairs on pond skaters' feet repel water and their six legs spread the insects' weight, helping them to whizz about on the surface. We want a go!

These carnivorous insects have a clever way of finding other bugs to eat, too. They use sensitive hairs on their legs to pick up movement in the water made by prey. So, if an insect falls into the water, the pond skater's legs detect vibrations and it moves in for the kill!

MEGA MOUND ▶

The tallest termite mound ever was found in the Republic of Congo and stood an unbelievable 12.8m high! That's as tall as an extinct Brachiosaurus!

AMAZING
BUG CITIES

Forget man-made skyscrapers – insects build the most spectacular structures on Earth! Known as social insects, these brilliant bug builders construct huge, complex nests and live together inside in large groups called colonies...

INSIDE A TERMITE MOUND

Cool colonies

All ants and termites, plus some bees and wasps, are social insects and live together in colonies. Each group has a queen, who controls how things are run, and all of the insects in the colony work together. These impressive groups are also home to different generations of insects, with new members regularly being born to take over from older ones and join the colony's workforce.

TERMITE

HONEYBEE

WASP

ANT

Dream teams

Social insects are great team players. Each insect has its own job, including building and maintaining the nest, reproduction, finding food and looking after eggs and young insects. Plus, with so many bugs living together, there's strength in numbers – these huge groups are awesome at defending their homes from predators!

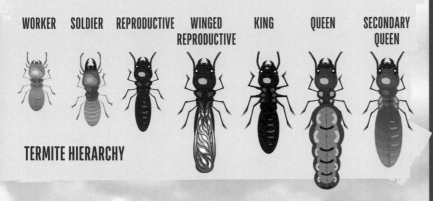

WORKER SOLDIER REPRODUCTIVE WINGED REPRODUCTIVE KING QUEEN SECONDARY QUEEN

TERMITE HIERARCHY

Epic navigation

Some insects, such as ants and bees, have an amazing magnetic sense. When they need to explore the area around their colony, they use the Earth's geomagnetic field to find their way home again! That must come in handy when members head out looking for food!

INSIDE AN ANT COLONY

SOLITARY STARS

Not all insects live in colonies. Some bugs – known as solitary insects – live on their own and don't usually interact with others. Here are three independent insects...

SPIDER WASP

1 Solitary wasp species feed on nectar and are often seen around flowers. These brilliant buzzers include spider wasps, jewel wasps and bee wolf wasps.

MASON BEE

2 Many bees are solitary insects, living in individual nests and working alone. Solitary bees include mason bees, plasterer bees and digger bees.

PRAYING MANTIS

3 The praying mantis is also a solitary bug. These crafty critters are deadly predators, using their quick reflexes and front legs to catch unsuspecting prey.

SWARM!

When bugs and insects get together, it can be bad news for crops!
But look within these social storms and you'll see that swarming is
a vital method of staying alive for insects

A **GROUP OF BUTTERFLIES** IS OFFICIALLY CALLED A **KALEIDOSCOPE**!

CATERPILLARS ARE AN **ARMY**

Strength in numbers

All sorts of insect species swarm – from ants, to
honeybees, to termites, to butterflies – but why?
Humans have found that teaming up is a great way
to get the job done and it's the same in the insect
world! Locusts swarm on food-finding missions, while
mosquitoes are on the hunt for a mate. Put enough of
any species together and they're likely to couple up –
for mosquitoes, it can be in the millions!

INVASION!

Group effort

How do insects do it? Humans might plan to meet up, but some species rely on stigmergy. Tiny actions leave a trace, which the next insect in line can copy without thinking – it's a reflex that seems smarter than it is! When they're out of the reach of their queen, flying ants fire out special chemicals called pheromones to stick together. Honeybees have smaller swarms, but scout bees streak through buzzing swarms to point the way home.

Hop along

In 2014, weather services in Albuquerque in America found a group of grasshoppers so big, they thought it was an actual storm! The short-horned grasshopper holds the record for having the biggest swarm – when they run out of food in one place, they'll feed on farmers' produce and anything else in their path! Causing chaos to crops, there can be up to 300 tons of these flying pests in just one square kilometre!

FAST⚡FACTS

1 Scientists have been trying to crack swarm intelligence using complex maths since the 1980s. By predicting the random actions of insects, there's hope they can control and work with pests.

2 Swarms have been bad news for crop owners for a long time! In the Bible's book of Exodus, locusts were the eighth plague suffered by the ancient Egyptians. They were said to 'eat every tree'!

3 In 1954, swarms of the desert locust Schistocerca gregaria whipped up a storm of a swarm in Kenya, covering 200 square kilometres. There were 50 billion insects in total!

CHAPTER 2

UP CLOSE WITH CREEPY-CRAWLIES!

Now we know what makes an insect an insect, it's time to get face-to-freaky-face with some of the world's most extraordinary, unusual and important bug species...

ANCIENT INSECTS

Compared to these creepy-crawlies, humans have been around for the blink of an eye – just 300,000 years! Insects have always been the real rulers of the planet. Here are some of the most astonishing old-school arthropods...

Long gone

These ancient insects were massive! So why did they get smaller? Most of the creatures featured here are from the Carboniferous period – a time 300 million years ago when plants were super-effective at pumping out oxygen. This oxygen-rich atmosphere meant there was less limit on the size of life, and insects reached record-breaking sizes!

This was the age when giant ancestors of the dragonfly – called griffinflies – ruled the skies! Found in France, the prehistoric dragonfly Meganeura Monyi is officially the largest insect ever, with a wingspan of 70cm!

Eventually, as the first birds evolved to be quicker and more agile, giant insects were hunted and knocked off the top of the food chain. Fossils show they gradually became smaller until they reached the sizes they are today. Thank goodness for that!

What's an arthropod?

Arthropods are armoured animals without a backbone whose shells are cleverly connected to help them move more easily. Insects, spiders, centipedes, millipedes, lobsters and crabs are all members of the arthropod family.

HALLUCIGENIA SPARSA

When a creature's been extinct for 400 million years, it can be hard to piece it together! And with the Hallucigenia sparsa, the more that scientists learn, the stranger it seems. Most closely related to today's vivid velvet worm, this baffling bottom feeder didn't just have defensive spines on its back, it had teeth in its throat. Where's its mouth?!

EURYPTERID

This sea scorpion was hefty enough to take down a horse! At 2.5m long, the eurypterid was longer than a table and crushed its dinner to death with 45cm claws! Laying in wait underwater, it blended into the sand and sediment, waiting to strike. Scientists think it would've torn its prey apart and then scavenged for scraps.

FACT SCIENTISTS HAVE RECREATED OXYGEN-BOOSTED ENVIRONMENTS AND HAVE PROVED THAT MORE AIR MEANS BIGGER BUGS.

BATTLING A DUNKLEOSTEUS!

ANOMALOCARIS

It's much safer to go swimming today than it was 500 million years ago! The Anomalocaris was a colossal crustacean that scoured oceans in search of a meal. Growing up to a metre in length, it used its wings and tail to boost through the water at shocking speeds. Scientists are still finding fossils of other species with bits missing – not broken off, but chomped by the Anomalocaris!

1 METRE LONG

A dive inside A BEE HIVE

With over 20,000 different species of bee, these buzzing bugs can be found all over the world apart from Antarctica! Most live in small families, but some group together in colonies, building amazing hives to live in. Want to take a look inside?

Hive home

Honeybees build their hives (or nests) in hollow trees, rock crevices and caves. Sometimes in warmer climates they create free-hanging, exposed nests on the branches of trees. Today some honeybees are kept in man-made structures, called beehives. People have collected honey from hives for thousands of years!

WORKER BEES

These are the colony's busiest bees. Worker bees are all female and they do all of the work in the hive. Their roles include building and guarding the hive, feeding the queen and other bees and foraging for food (pollen and nectar from flowers). Worker bees live for around six weeks and they're the ones you see flying about near a hive.

QUEEN

One queen is in charge of the whole hive! Queens are chosen when they're still eggs and are fed special food, called royal jelly. This nutrient-rich food is what helps the bee become a fertile queen. The queen's job is to lay eggs for the hive's next generation of bees, and she can lay up to 2,500 eggs in one day! The queen also guides the behaviour of the bees in her colony by releasing special chemicals. Queen bees can live for up to five years.

The bees use a hexagonal pattern because it makes the structure stronger and means they can store as much honey as possible. Clever!

3 When the construction is finished, the nest will have one entrance and will last for around two years. The top cells of the nest will store honey and pollen, with worker cells underneath and then drone cells. The queen bee has her own special cells at the bottom of the nest!

BUILDING BEES

So, how do honeybees build a new nest? It's a complex, clever process!

1 Once a safe place for a new nest has been chosen, worker bees begin by covering the walls with a layer of propolis, a red/brown substance they collect from plants and tree buds. This bee glue is great for filling in tiny gaps or draughty cracks and it also helps protect the colony from germs.

2 Next, worker bees get going on the structure, which they build with a wax they produce themselves. Their bodies contain glands that convert honey into wax, which then oozes through the bee's abdomen and is collected and chewed by other bees. This makes the wax softer so it can be used to fill the nest with neat hexagonal (six-sided) cells.

DRONES

Each colony has a few hundred male honey bees, called drones. The drones' purpose is to mate with the queen so she can lay fertilised eggs, which develop into new bees. Drones live for around 12 weeks.

FAST⚡FACTS

1 There are 100 female worker bees for every male drone!

2 As well as delicious honey, honeybees also produce beeswax, which people use to make candles, polish and even types of paint.

HEY, HONEY

1

A scout honeybee leaves the hive to forage for flowers that contain sweet liquid nectar, the main ingredient for honey and the main energy source for all bees. Once located, the honeybee flies back to its colony to pass on the word to the other bees, using a special waggle dance.

2

Honeybees use their straw-like proboscis to suck up the nectar droplets produced by the flowers, usually in the centre of the flower but also in its stems and leaves.

COUNT THEM

Honeybees have two stomachs! They use one for eating and the other honey stomach to carry precious nectar or water back to their hive. Amazingly, they have five eyes – two large compound eyes and three smaller eyes in the centre of their heads, known as ocelli. They have four wings in total, with the rear and front ones hooking together for flight and unhooking easily afterwards.

OCELLI

HONEY STOMACH

STOMACH

Powerful pollinators

Bees are essential to our ecosystem. That's because they collect pollen on special hairs on their back legs called scopa when they flit between flowers. Pollen is a powder which trees, grasses and flowering plants make and must spread to multiply. Incredibly, about one third of the food we eat is pollinated by bees!

Only the honeybee makes the sweet, delicious honey we eat. These clever bees produce honey to store in the hive to feed themselves during the colder months when there aren't as many flowers to gather food from. Let's follow the honey trail...

3

When the nectar reaches the bee's honey stomach, it begins to break down the complex sugars of the nectar into more simple sugars to stop them crystallising or becoming solid in a process called inversion.

4

It's teamwork all the way back at the hive, where the nectar is passed mouth to mouth by house bees who each chew on it for about 30 minutes, slowly turning it into tasty honey!

5

Then it's time to store the honey ready for the winter, in the hexagon-shaped wax honeycomb cells at the top of the hive. To make the honey thicker and more like syrup, the bees beat their wings rapidly over it. Finally, they pop on a little wax lid to seal it. How clever is that?

6

A beekeeper removes some of the honey, being careful not to damage the hive and leaving enough for the hard-working bees. When the bees are hungry, they open the little jars and share their sweet treasure. Thanks, bees!

BRILLIANT
BEETLES

With a whopping 350,000 to 400,000 known species, beetles are the biggest insect group. In fact, almost half of all the planet's insects are beetles. They're designed to survive!

▲ A stunningly shiny jewel beetle, or metallic wood-boring beetle

▲ The Siamese rhinoceros beetle is famous for its fearsome fighting skills, but it's no slouch at flying, either!

Winged wonders

Beetles belong to the insect order Coleoptera. They're found all over the world in nearly every habitat, making them Earth's most diverse group of insects. Their name means 'sheath-winged' in Greek because they have two sets of wings. The front outer pair – called elytra – are leathery wing cases and cover a second softer set of hind wings, which are used for flight. These flight wings are safely folded away when they're not in use.

BEETLE BENEFITS

Beetles are incredibly important to the health of our planet. Here are five reasons why...

1 Some beetles, such as soldier beetles and blister beetles, are pollinators, helping to spread pollen from flower to flower.

2 Like a lot of other insects, beetles are a food source for lots of animals.

3 Beetles help keep things tidy, feeding on leaf litter and weeds and even dead animals.

4 Certain beetles, such as bombardier beetles, are insectivores (animals that eat insects) and feed on problem bugs that destroy crops.

5 Carrion beetles and longhorn beetles are decomposers and help to keep soil healthy by breaking down organic matter.

Common red soldier beetles love eating aphids and pollen

An adult false bombardier beetle feasting on a moth

Grow for it!

Like many insects, beetles change as they grow, with young larvae looking very different to adults. Beetles are holometabolous insects, which means they go through four different stages: egg, larva, pupa and adult.

▶ This is the complete growth (metamorphosis) of the jewel beetle – from an egg less than a millimetre in size to 6.5cm in some adults

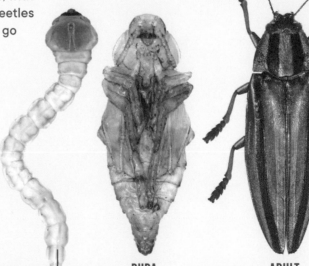

EGG   LARVA   PUPA   ADULT

Violin beetle

This beetle is named after its front legs, which are shaped like a violin. It grows up to 10cm long and feeds on other insects and snails.

BEETLES MAKE UP 25% OF ALL ANIMALS ON THE PLANET!

Great diving beetle

These beetles are found in ponds and streams in Europe and Northern Asia. They grow up to 4cm long and eat tadpoles, other insects, worms and even small fish. Great diving beetles store air beneath their wing-cases when they swim and use their back legs to guide them like a pair of oars!

It's thought the hairy jewel beetle collects pollen on its back to camouflage itself from predators. So sneaky!

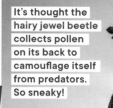

Hercules beetle

Found in Central and South America, the Hercules beetle is one of the world's biggest beetles, growing up to 19cm long! Its elytra (front wing-casings) change colour with the weather – if it's dry they're going to be yellow or green and if it's humid they turn black!

TAKE OFF!

THE LOWDOWN ON LADYBIRDS

✳ Also known as ladybugs or lady beetles, there are around 5,000 different species of ladybirds.

✳ Not all ladybirds are red and black – they come in lots of different colours and patterns.

✳ Ladybirds aren't poisonous to humans but they can have toxic effects on small animals.

✳ Ladybirds' brightly coloured bodies act as a warning to predators – such as birds, wasps and dragonflies – not to eat them, as they could be poisonous. It's an effective trick!

✳ Ladybirds usually live for a year.

✳ These insects help protect farmers' crops by eating aphids and other pests. One ladybird can eat up to 5,000 aphids in its lifetime!

✳ If a ladybird feels threatened, it releases a smelly yellow fluid from its legs to put off any hungry predators. Pee-ew!

▲ The 22-spot yellow ladybird has distinct rounded dots that never blend together

▲ A ladybird chewing on an aphid. You can encourage more to visit you by creating a simple ladybird hotel from a few pine cones bound together with twine!

MEET THE
DUNG BEETLE

Nature always has a way of surprising us! Take dung beetles – there are over 5,000 species of these insects and they just can't get enough of animal poo! Eating it, rolling it and building houses from it – dung beetles put the waste from other animals to good use everywhere except Antarctica

HOW THEY ROLL

There are three main dung beetle groups...

1 ROLLERS shape parcels of animal dung into balls and roll them away from the poo pile before burying them to snack on later. Sometimes females lay their eggs on them, in which case they're known as brood balls. Males are expert rollers thanks to the spurs on their powerful back legs, which spike into the balls. Rollers need their wits about them to stop other cheeky dung beetles stealing their balls!

2 DWELLERS dive straight into the poo, making themselves right at home! You'll often find pupa here, little sacks which have developed from the eggs laid by the female, getting ready to undergo a transformation – or metamorphosis – into a baby beetle.

3 TUNNELLERS dig into the ground underneath the dung pile with their super-strong front legs to stash their dung ball.

THE AVERAGE LIFE SPAN OF A DUNG BEETLE IS AROUND THREE TO FIVE YEARS

What's on the menu?

Well, it's not quite as gross as you'd think. When an animal – and that includes us humans – eats food, there are parts of it that don't get digested and that's what comes out as poo. This is what dung beetles go for, with their young or larvae eating the solid part and the adults drinking up the nutritious moisture found in the juicy liquid. Yum!

Dung beetles do have some standards, though! Most pick dung made by herbivores – animals that only eat plants. Elephants on the plains of Africa are herbivores, for example, grazing on grass, twigs and flowers. Other herbivores are deer, cows and camels.

Some dung beetles use their acute sense of smell to follow the scent of poo produced by omnivores – animals that eat both plants and meat, such as bears.

MALE DUNG BEETLES SOMETIMES FIGHT, LOCKING HORNS TO COMPETE FOR FEMALES

▲ A close-up of South African dung beetles, also known as tunnellers, diving into the freshest hot manure from an elephant

A roller can pull an incredible 1,141 times its own bodyweight, making it one of the world's strongest animals in relation to its size. That's the same as a human pulling six double decker buses – filled with passengers, not poo! – along a road.

HEAVE-HO!

FAST⚡FACTS

1 Scientists have discovered that a super-clever African species, Scarabaeus satyrus, looks to the stars in the Milky Way to show them their way home!

2 To make a swift getaway, a dung beetle can fly using its wings, which create a loud buzzing sound as they beat quickly through the air.

3 Dung beetles can grow up to 17cm as adults and weigh up to 100g.

4 Dung beetles have six legs and, in some species, the male has a long, curved horn on its head. Perfect for spearing those stool samples!

BEAUTIFUL BUTTERFLIES

The sight of a colourful butterfly flitting happily on a sunny day is sure to make you smile. But these flying insects began life as something completely different...

LIFE CYCLE OF A BUTTERFLY

How a monarch butterfly takes shape...

Stage 1
THE EGG

The female butterfly lays up to 300 sticky eggs on leaves or plants. While these eggs can differ – round or cylindrical, smooth or wrinkled, depending on the species – they're where tiny caterpillars start to grow and change!

Stage 2
THE CATERPILLAR

Around six to eight days later, the caterpillar is so hungry, it eats its way out of the egg and chomps on the surrounding leaf. As it supersizes, a caterpillar can shed its skin four or five times, and a fully-grown one can be over 100 times larger at the end of the process, which can last for up to a month!

◀ Monarch caterpillars hatch from their egg and then eat it

Stage 3
THE PUPA

The pupa, or chrysalis, is a hanging vessel spun by the caterpillar around itself and where the transformation happens. This stage can last for a few weeks to several months and a hardened case, a bit like armour, forms around the pupa to protect the vulnerable caterpillar from predators and harsh weather. Inside, new tissue, limbs and organs grow...

Stage 4
THE BUTTERFLY

The chrysalis cracks open to reveal the miraculous metamorphosis as the butterfly emerges. However, its wings are crinkled and wet after being squished inside, so it patiently lets them dry out and makes them strong by pumping a liquid called hemolymph into them before taking its first flight.

The marvel of wings

A butterfly has four wings, two on each side, which move in a figure of eight pattern during flight. Their wings are made up of two fine chitinous layers, or membranes, and under a powerful microscope you'd see thousands of tiny scales and hairs.

 EYESPOTS

◀ Buckeye butterfly

FOREWING

HIND WING

Along with moths, butterflies are the only scale-winged insects. Wings are breathing parts of the butterfly, supplied by oxygen through tiny veins. Eyespots on some wings mimic the faces of bigger animals, such as owls, to fool predators, while other species, such as the Australian leafwing butterfly, are shaped like leaves to avoid detection.

Australian leafwing butterfly

Environmental angels

Like bees, butterflies feed on nectar and are attracted to all the bright flowers in gardens and meadows. They also collect pollen, spreading it to other flowers and helping them to reproduce, which is vital for the ecosystem. Scientists are closely monitoring our butterfly population, which is super-sensitive to habitat and climate change.

▶ Monarch butterflies don't eat like us but instead sip nectar through a straw-like tube called a proboscis

HOW TO MAKE A BUTTERFLY FEEDER

You will need:
* A plastic lid from a large empty yoghurt pot
* A hole punch
* String or yarn, cut into 6 x 30cm lengths
* Scissors
* Over-ripe fruit, cut into slices
* A helpful adult!

What to do:
1 Use the hole punch to make equally spaced holes in the inside rim of the plastic lid.
2 Loop and secure the string through and tie them all together at the top, attaching the artificial flowers.
3 Place the fruit on the lid and then attach the feeder to the branch of a tree. How many butterflies can you spot?

SUPER FLY GUYS

The flight of the dragonfly is so special that engineers have spent years trying to copy it. Well, as one of the first winged insects to evolve, they've had 300 million years to practise! More than 5,000 species of dragonfly really can hover like helicopters. Let's meet these awesome aviators

Incredible flying machines

Dragonflies aren't actually flies because they have four wings instead of two. And unlike other insects, they beat their wings up and down, rather than backwards and forwards. A dragonfly can move each wing, which is made from a complex map of veins held together by a shiny film called chitin, separately, using muscles below its exoskeleton. To perform their acrobatic moves, they're helped by a pterostigma on each wing, which act like weights to keep the ultrafine wings steady. When it's time to chill out, a dragonflies' wings stand out sideways and don't fold inwards like those of a butterfly.

THE SMALLEST DRAGONFLIES HAVE WINGSPANS OF ABOUT 2CM, WITH THE LARGEST UP TO 15CM!

DRAGONFLIES CAN **REACH** SPEEDS OF

48KM/H

15CM

2CM

FAST⚡FACT

Ancient dragonfly fossils have been discovered with wingspans of up to 60cm.

My, what big eyes you have!

A dragonfly's two compound eyes are huge in comparison to the size of its head. If you were a dragonfly, your eyes would be the size of a football helmet! Each of these globe-like eyes are covered in up to 30,000 telescope-shaped lenses or ommatidia, which gather information and give the dragonfly a nearly 360° field of vision. They do have a blind spot, however: right behind them. Unlike human eyes, compound eyes can't change focus, so dragonflies can only see objects close to them in clear detail. Dragonflies have binocular vision to help them accurately judge distances – essential for catching their next tasty meal!

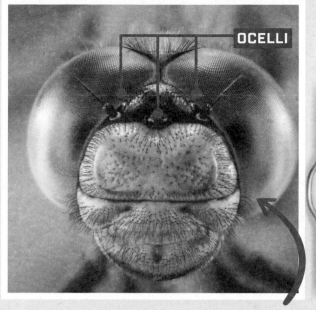

OCELLI

▶ Every single one of these lenses is picking up an incredible amount of data!

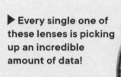

Dragonflies also have an extra three eyes!
Called ocelli, they're located behind the compound eyes. It's thought these light-sensitive 'simple' eyes are used to help the insect work out when it's day or night.

All the colours

You have tri-chromatic vision, meaning you see colours as a mix of red, blue and green. This is due to the three light-sensitive proteins called opsins in your eyes. Most animals have either di (two), tri (three) or tetra (four) chromatic vision. But some dragonflies see the world in ultra-multicolour because they have 30 different opsins.

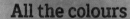

Let us prey!

You'll find dragonflies close to bodies of water around the world. And their impressive flying skills are key to their survival – without them, they'd starve. Scientific tests show that a dragonfly captures around 95% of its prey, eating small insects such as flies and mosquitoes mid-air, using their serrated saw-like teeth. For larger snacks, such as small butterflies, a hungry dragonfly creates a basket using some of its six legs to scoop up the insect and whisk it to a nearby perch.

AMAZING SPIDER FACTS

Think you know all about spiders? Think again! From super-strength and size to huge fangs and silky slingshots, read on for ten mind-boggling facts about these astonishing arachnids

You might think the European garden spider is just sitting pretty, but it's ready to strike at any second!

1 Spiders aren't insects

Along with scorpions, mites and ticks, spiders are part of a group of animals called arachnids. There are 65,000 arachnid species and around half of them are thought to be spiders.

Arachnids are different from insects in a few ways – unlike insects, arachnids have eight legs and their bodies are split into two parts (insect bodies have three sections). Plus, arachnids have six or eight eyes, while insects have two.

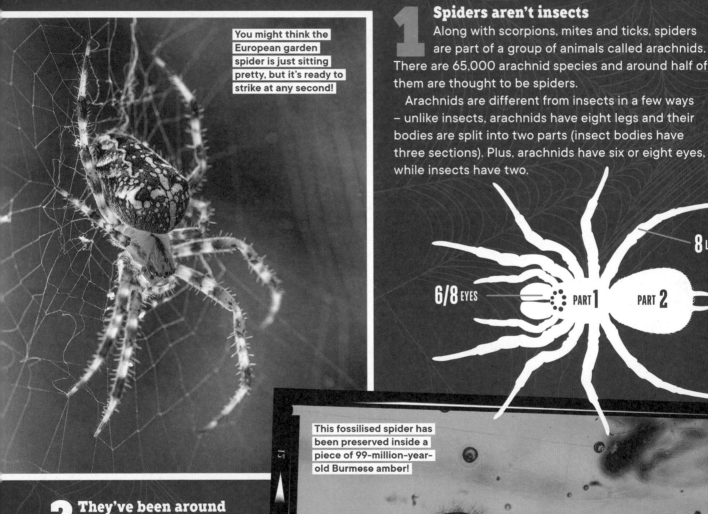

8 LEGS

6/8 EYES   PART 1   PART 2

This fossilised spider has been preserved inside a piece of 99-million-year-old Burmese amber!

2 They've been around a very long time

Fossil evidence found in a French town called Montceau-les-Mines reveals spiders have been around for at least 305 million years! A spider-like creature was also discovered alongside the ancient spider fossil, helping researchers understand how spiders evolved.

3 They come in all shapes and sizes

Not all spiders are black and hairy. Some, such as the Samoan moss spider, are the size of a full stop, while others – including giant huntsman spiders – are as big as a dinner plate!

The world's heaviest spider, the goliath tarantula, lives in South America and can weigh up to 175g – as much as three tennis balls!

ACTUAL SIZE

GOLIATH TARANTULA HAS FANGS AROUND 2.5CM LONG

GOLIATH SPIDERS ARE SO BIG THAT EVEN BIRDS ARE ON THE MENU!

4 Spiders spin thread as strong as steel

Spiders spin sticky silk threads, which they use to build webs to trap prey, line their burrows and protect their eggs. Spider silk is one of the strongest natural materials on Earth – compared to a steel thread of the same weight, spider silk is stronger and tougher!

5 They have blue blood!

Human blood is based around a protein called haemoglobin that allows red blood cells to carry oxygen around the body. Haemoglobin contains iron which is why it's red. Around a spider's body, oxygen is transported by a protein called haemocyanin, which contains copper and makes its blood look blue!

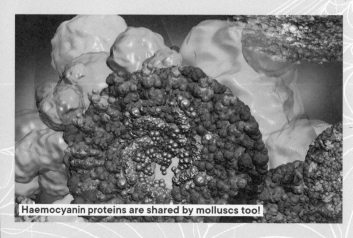

Haemocyanin proteins are shared by molluscs too!

6 No muscles? No problem!

Most animals with limbs use muscles to move about but spiders rely on something called hydraulic power. This is because their legs are missing muscles to pull them outwards. Spiders get round this and move their spindly limbs by shifting their body's internal fluids around. Doing this increases pressure in their midsections, which makes their legs stretch outwards! So spiders walk by quickly increasing and decreasing the pressure in their bodies to make their legs move. And if they want to jump? A sudden burst of pressure will make their legs snap outwards and launch them into the air!

7 They're recycling stars!

If a spider's web is damaged, becomes dirty or loses its stickiness, some species of spider, such as orb-weavers, recycle it! Wind and rain can damage the structure of a spider's web and dust and pollen can stop the silk from being sticky, making it less likely to catch prey. So the spider recycles its web by rolling the threads into a ball and eating it. This allows the spider to reuse the nutrients in the silk so they can make a fresh new web!

◀ A spiny orb-weaver ready to feast on wasted webs

8 They can move super-fast!

The fastest spider on Earth is thought to be the Moroccan flic-flac spider. This desert-dweller uses a special rolling motion – a bit like the movements used by acrobatic circus tumblers – to reach speeds of up to 1.7 metres per second.

The Peruvian triangle weaver spider is another speedy arachnid. This creepy-crawly uses its web as a slingshot – and fires itself towards tasty-looking prey! As it flies forwards, the spider moves at up to 60 times the acceleration of a sprinting cheetah!

THE FLIC-FLAC SPIDER **CAN RUN UP TO** **1.7** METRES PER **SECOND**

9 Spiders are hunting heroes!

The world's spiders eat 400 to 800 billion kilograms of insects every year – that's the same weight as 15,000 to 30,000 Statues of Liberty! They accomplish this by being pretty inventive predators...

Bolas spiders catch male moths by making a ball of sticky silk, which smells like a female moth. They hang it from a single line and their bait lures unsuspecting male moths like a fishing rod. Hook, line and sinker!

Wall spiders run round their prey – which is often an ant – and wrap their victim in one long silk cord. Once the prey is trapped, the spider goes in for the kill. It's like being mummified... alive!

Spitting spiders spew a disgusting, gooey substance from their mouthparts at potential prey. When the special spider-glue hits, it shrinks and traps prey in place, like a statue.

STRONG SPIDER!

CALIFORNIA TRAPDOOR SPIDER RESISTS FORCE 38 TIMES ITS SIZE

10 They can be seriously strong

They may be small but spiders can be really powerful. The world's strongest spider is the California trapdoor spider. It gets its name from the way it covers the entrance to its underground burrow, which is like a trapdoor. When it senses danger, this spider hides in its burrow and holds the door shut with its mouth and claws. The creepy-crawly is so strong, it can resist a force 38 times its own bodyweight, which is like a man holding a door closed when it's being pulled by a small jet plane. Don't try it at home!

BE A SPIDER FRIEND!

Check the bath
Spiders are just like us – they need to drink too, which is why they're often in the bathroom. Don't wash them down the plughole! Instead, if it's safe to do so, remove them before you turn on the taps and then enjoy your soak in peace.

Don't kill crawly critters
Some spiders are at risk of extinction and need our help to survive. If you really can't live with a spider in plain sight, trap it safely and release it somewhere suitable, where it can continue as part of the ecosystem.

Face your fear
If you'd like to overcome a fear of spiders, sanctuaries and zoos are the perfect place to get up close and personal safely.

TARANTULA!

Did you know that there are tarantula beauty contests? While most spider species are unremarkable shades of brown and black, some stand out from the crowd, thanks to their jewel-bright colours, delicate patterns and fluffy appearance. Don't believe us? Then roll up, roll up for the world's greatest tarantula beauty show!

MEXICAN FIRELEG →

WHERE? **Southern and Western Mexico**

With its fiery-coloured legs, which start out as a bright rusty red before fading to orange, the Mexican fireleg is seriously striking. But this nervous tarantula doesn't show off, instead preferring to burrow into the subtropical Mexican forest ground. While its fuzzy hair makes it look adorable, it has a purpose – vibrating to let the spider know when a potential yummy insect meal is close by. Mexican firelegs also urticate, defending themselves by firing a mist of microscopic, barbed hairs at an enemy. Yikes!

← ANTILLES PINKTOE

WHERE? **Martinique, Caribbean**

Sometimes called the Martinique red tree spider, as a sling or young spider, the Antilles pinktoe has a metallic blue-black appearance, before growing into its gorgeous colours as an adult. The shiny green-blue carapace (bony shield) acts as a protective shell and the spider's legs grow furry coats in reds, browns and pinks. Its long legs help it to jump distances of up to 30cm and the Antilles pinktoe is known for its chilled-out personality!

← GREENBOTTLE BLUE

WHERE? Venezuela, South America

The contrast of the bright orange tummy with the metallic blue-green body and legs of the Greenbottle blue make it a wonder to see. Its colours change as it gets older, apart from its little black boots. Cute! This clever tarantula creates intricate webbed hammocks and tunnels in the tree roots and bushes of the Venezuelan desert and is also known to weave complex funnels to protect itself from the harsh climate and to trap tasty morsels to eat such as worms and crickets. These little fellas are quite shy, scurrying off at the first sign of danger.

GOOTY SAPPHIRE TARANTULA →

WHERE? India

Scientists still can't decide whether the extraordinary cobalt blue colouring of the Gooty sapphire tarantula acts as a warning to other creatures to keep their distance or if it's a way to attract a mate. What we do know is that these critically endangered spiders live in holes of tall trees in India's Andhra Pradesh region – trees that are chopped down for firewood and logging. Luckily, these spiders have an impressive jump and can also float down to the forest floor, leading to their other name, the Peacock parachute spider!

← ORANGE BABOON

WHERE? South Africa, Angola, Kenya, Zimbabwe, Tanzania, Mozambique and Malawi

This species is also known as the Mombasa golden starburst tarantula thanks to its gorgeous carapace markings. It's also called the OBT – orange bitey thing! That's because it is an old world tarantula. These species from the eastern hemisphere sink their little fangs into an enemy and their venom is stronger than that of a new world tarantula (those found in the western hemisphere). When it adopts a threat posture, raising its front legs and baring its fangs, it's time to leg it!

SUPER SCORPIONS

There's a sting in the 'tale' of what you think you know about scorpions! As members of the arachnid family – they count spiders and mites as relatives – there are around 1,500 different kinds living mainly in desert climates around the world. But only 25 species are potentially deadly to people

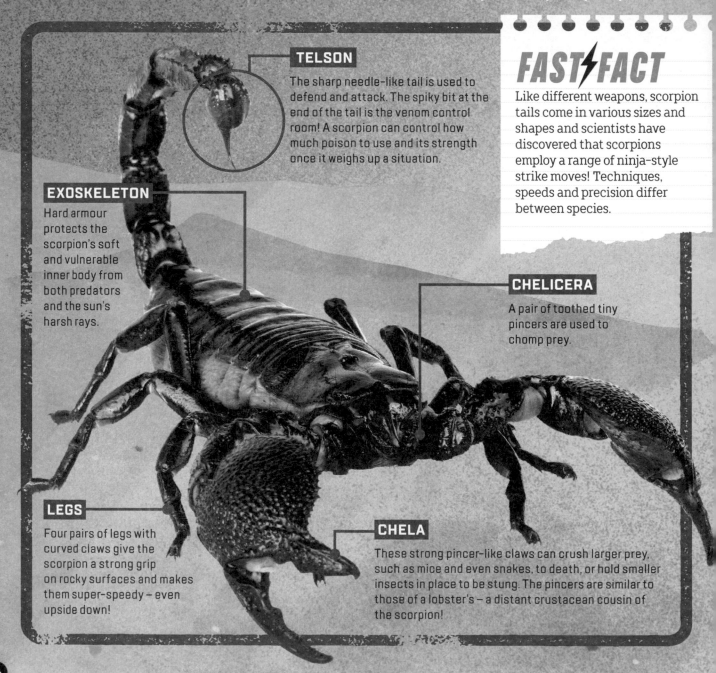

TELSON

The sharp needle-like tail is used to defend and attack. The spiky bit at the end of the tail is the venom control room! A scorpion can control how much poison to use and its strength once it weighs up a situation.

EXOSKELETON

Hard armour protects the scorpion's soft and vulnerable inner body from both predators and the sun's harsh rays.

FAST⚡FACT

Like different weapons, scorpion tails come in various sizes and shapes and scientists have discovered that scorpions employ a range of ninja-style strike moves! Techniques, speeds and precision differ between species.

CHELICERA

A pair of toothed tiny pincers are used to chomp prey.

LEGS

Four pairs of legs with curved claws give the scorpion a strong grip on rocky surfaces and makes them super-speedy – even upside down!

CHELA

These strong pincer-like claws can crush larger prey, such as mice and even snakes, to death, or hold smaller insects in place to be stung. The pincers are similar to those of a lobster's – a distant crustacean cousin of the scorpion!

Lethal legend

Ever wondered what the story behind scorpio in the zodiac is? Sure, the stars that make up the constellation's scorpion shape might not really look like the real thing, but it's based on the legend that a scorpion finished off the giant Greek hunter Orion with its signature sting. There's also a story about ancient arachnids knocking the sun off its path. They've been considered dangerous for millennia!

Hitching a ride

In a practice known as viviparity, scorpions produce live babies! During gestation, or pregnancy, some develop within a membrane sack, while others are nourished directly from their mothers. At birth, the little ones – who are white – catch a ride on their mum's back for up to 50 days for protection and sustenance, until they moult or shed their skins for the first time.

BABY SCORPIONS DEVELOP FOR BETWEEN TWO TO 18 MONTHS

MATING GAMES!

Dance of death

Mating scorpions look a little like a man and a woman doing an old-fashioned waltz! Called the promenade à deux (a walk for two), the male grabs the female's pincers with his own and they shuffle backwards and forwards. It might look romantic, but after all that exercise, the female is hungry... and can sometimes try to eat the male afterwards. It's the deadliest dance routine ever!

▼ A scorpion and its baby eating a black widow spider

Table manners

You might not want a scorpion as a dinner guest! They use their chelicera mouthparts to chew on their prey, breaking down the soft parts of the meal with digestive fluids. Anything that is too hard to eat is discarded – gross!

SCORPIONS CAN EAT UP TO A THIRD OF THEIR OWN BODY WEIGHT IN ONE SNACKATHON!

MEGA CRAWLERS

With their many legs, centipedes and millipedes can give many of us the shivers! But these bugs are largely harmless to humans and the way they move is pretty cool. The crawling critters aren't insects because they have more than six legs, but they belong to the same arthropod family and are also related to spiders, crabs and lobsters. Both are invertebrates, meaning they have no spine. Let's put in the legwork to find out more

CENTIPEDE VS MILLIPEDE

It's time to squash... a myth! Many people think centipedes have 100 legs because centi means 100. Likewise, milli means 1,000, but centipedes and millipedes definitely don't have that many legs!

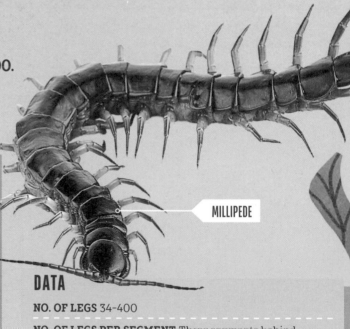

MILLIPEDE

DATA

NO. OF LEGS 15-30

NO. OF LEGS PER SEGMENT 1 pair, pointing outwards

LENGTH 1-30cm

ANTENNAE Short

NO. OF SPECIES Approx 8,000

HABITAT Loves dry environments, such as deserts, deep caves... and your home!

FOOD Carnivorous centipedes come out at night to eat smaller insects and bugs, moving swiftly to inject their next meal with venom from their forcipules

DATA

NO. OF LEGS 34-400

NO. OF LEGS PER SEGMENT Three segments behind the head have one pair each. All other segments have two pairs, pointing downwards

LENGTH 0.32-27 cm

ANTENNAE Long

NO. OF SPECIES Approx 10,000

HABITAT Loves damp environments, such as moist soil in dense forest.

FOOD Millipedes are scavengers and love to munch on anything that is decaying, such as tree roots, plant leaves and wild mushrooms.

CENTIPEDE

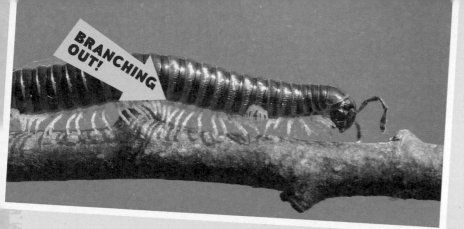

BRANCHING OUT!

Play detective

Have a scout around under the dead leaves or logs in your garden or nearest outdoor space. A centipede will run away immediately, while a millipede will curl up into a tight coil and play dead until you've moved on. If you get too close, a millipede might release an irritant or nasty chemical to protect itself.

Move it!

Millipedes move their jointed legs in a wave-like motion known as undulation, a little like a Mexican wave! They're slow coaches compared to centipedes, who can get pretty speedy by only undulating slightly while walking. Jointed centipede legs also grow in length towards the end of the body, which means there's more space between the legs immediately in front, helping them to move faster.

The giant African millipede, Archispirostreptus gigas, is the world's longest millipede, growing up to around 33cm in length – roughly the size of a laptop screen!

THIS BIG

Growing pains

You'll notice the lines on the bodies, or trunks, of centipedes and millipedes. Many of the species will hatch with a certain number of these segments, adding more each time they moult, shedding their hard outer covering! And if they're unlucky enough to cross paths with a predator and lose a leg or two, they can regenerate. However, the superpower to grow limbs back only lasts until they reach adulthood.

FAST FACTS

1 Fossils of centipedes have been found that show the arthropod has been walking the Earth for more than 400 million years – they're built to survive!

2 The giant desert centipede gives a bee-like sting. Leave it alone!

3 Both centipedes and millipedes can be found worldwide, with some tough-as-boots centipedes even surviving the unforgiving -60°C temperatures of the Arctic Circle!

STICK 'EM UP!

The stick insect is a true trickster! Blessed with one of nature's most effective camouflage systems, it blends in brilliantly with the bark, twigs and leaves of its forest home. Let's find out more about these sneaky sticks...

Oh baby!

Even before they're born, stick insects are disguised – the mother lays eggs that look like plant seeds. Before this, an extraordinary non-stop mating ritual happens for up to 79 days! After sniffing out a potential mate via chemicals in the air, the frisky male and female join and hold on tight for days or weeks so the male can fertilise the female's eggs. Incredibly, if a female can't find a male, she can reproduce on her own, creating mini versions of herself! Called parthenogenesis, scientists are still studying this amazing natural phenomenon.

EGGS LOOK LIKE A SEED!

ART OF CAMOUFLAGE

The stick insect's scientific name, Phasmatodea, comes from the Greek word phasma, or ghost, and reveals its SAS-style survival skill of being able to mimic a host plant by swaying in the breeze like leaves! Some exotic species even have fake buds and patches that look like lichen (a type of moss) to give enemies the slip.

◀ Some look like flattened leaves, all the better to 'disappear'

◀ Some have bold colours to signal to predators that they taste pretty yucky!

Several species even have wings ▼

Size it up

Stick insects are among the world's longest insects. The smallest is North America's Timema cristinae at just over 1.2cm long – the size of your pinkie! The largest is nearly 60 times that size! China's Phryganistria chinensis Zhao is double the length of a human foot!

1.2CM

THERE ARE AN ESTIMATED **3,000 SPECIES** OF STICK INSECTS AROUND THE WORLD

STICK INSECTS ARE **EXTREMELY SLOOOOOW** MOVING, ONLY TAKING **3 STEPS AT A TIME!**

A sticky situation

When predators approach a stick insect, it makes like a statue and stays still to blend in. But even if the little critter is unlucky and loses a leg, it doesn't matter because before they reach maturity, stick insects have the power to regenerate, or grow it back! Stick insects can also play dead for hours and swipe their enemies with sharp spines on their legs.

KICKIN' CICADAS

You'll hear cicadas, the world's loudest insects, way before you see them! It's all to do with the insect's extraordinary life cycle, which can mean they're stuck underground for up to 17 years! Can you imagine that? When they finally emerge for a few short weeks, they want the whole world – and potential mates – to know!

Stage 1

EGG-STRAORDINARY!

There are three stages in the life cycle of a cicada – eggs, nymphs and adults. First, the female lays around 400 rice-shaped eggs inside twigs and branches, where they remain for between 6-10 weeks before hatching as tiny white ant-like insects and slurping on the sap (the juice) of the tree.

Stage 2

MAKING THE LEAP

The little nymph falls all the way down to the forest floor and burrows underground to carry on sucking up all the liquidy goodness found in the roots of the tree. Cicadas are busy underground, tunnelling and feeding – not sleeping or hibernating as scientists used to think they did.

Stage 3

COMING UP!

After between 2-17 years (yikes!), cicadas emerge from the ground as nymphs. They clamber up the nearest plant and undergo a metamorphosis, shedding their old skin. Wings emerge and are flooded with power-giving haemolymph fluid. Its new skin hardens, ready to take on the big wide world.

MOST NOISES CICADAS MAKE GO UP TO 100 DECIBELS. THAT'S THE SAME VOLUME AS A CHAINSAW!

Make a racket

Adult cicadas, or imagoes, have around four to six weeks to mate before dying. That's why they're so noisy! Males 'sing' by flexing their tymbals, which are drum-like organs found in their abdomens. Small muscles make the tymbals pulsate and the sound is intensified by the cicada's mostly hollow abdomen. The females signal their interest by flicking their wings to make a clicking sound, which sounds similar to clicking your fingers. Snap!

There are more than 3,400 known species of cicadas with one thing in common – they emerge in the summer in the mood for lurrrve! There are annual cicadas that pop up every year and periodical cicadas that only bask in the sun's warmth once every decade or two. Depending on where they are in the world, periodical cicadas generally have 13 or 17-year brood cycles. The Magicicada species has been documented to emerge after 22 years in US states including Tennessee and Ohio. For a bug, that's a long time!

Where in the world?

Cicadas live all over the globe but most species of these loud lovers are unique to North America.

The world's loudest cicada is the Brevisana brevis, an insect found in Africa that reaches **106.7 decibels** when recorded from 50cm away. That's louder than a hammer drill!

Wings of gold

The beautiful Tacua speciosa has been spotted in Malaysia and Indonesia and the islands of Borneo and Sumatra. It has opaque wings marked with gold veins and a striking yellow collar!

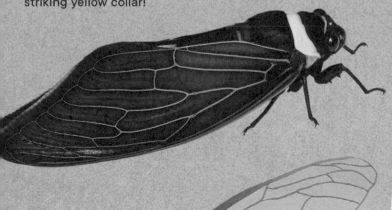

The world's largest species of cicada is Malaysia's Megapomponia imperatoria – it's about 7cm!

RECORD BREAKING BUGS

There might be more than a million species of bugs and insects alive on the planet – but these record breakers leap higher and fly further than any others!

TSETSE FLY

Rwanda

When it comes to bloodsucking, the tsetse fly is neck and neck with the mosquito! Dwelling in damp spots in the African Sahara, tsetse flies are about the size of a horsefly. They can consume up to three times their own bodyweight in blood in one go and considering they can each live up to four months, that's a lot of blood to suck up in one lifetime!

For these tiny vampires much bigger animals are on the menu and they have been for a long time – scientists have found fossils in Colorado dating back 34 million years. There are 24 species of tsetse fly and their ability to suck blood from humans, cattle, horses and pigs means they transmit deadly diseases. Unlike other parasitic species, it doesn't seem like the tsetse fly is trying to kill us... it's just trying to get full. What does it need all that blood for? Buzzing around is thirsty work, and the females turn it into milk for their babies.

BLOODIEST BUG
100% blood diet

MONARCH BUTTERFLY

PAINTED LADY BUTTERFLY

DESERT LOCUST

FURTHEST MIGRATION
6,000km

THE GLOBE SKIMMER DRAGONFLY IS **FEATURED** ON

POSTAGE STAMPS

AROUND THE WORLD BECAUSE OF ITS WIDE DISTRIBUTION!

GLOBE SKIMMER
India

We've known about this winged wanderer since the 1790s, but it's only recently been discovered to be a globetrotting explorer! Also known as the wandering glider, this dragonfly is a brutal hunter and it's known to rip the wings off its prey in mid-air... yikes! It's the most widespread of its kind on the planet – considering just how far globe skimmers go to survive, it's not surprising. Different generations join to make a tandem journey every year, covering up to 18,000km on their quest – these tiny travellers are only 4.5cm long, but their mission is much, much bigger.

Flying at five metres per second, globe skimmers brave nasty weather to stay in the right climate and eat a never-ending stream of tasty prey on their travels, from shrimps to tadpoles. Because so much of their journey is over open water a lot of their diet ends up being aquatic! Globe skimmers are incredible at using the environment to their advantage. Just like birds migrate, they stock up on fats and use wind trajectory to propel them forwards! Human drone builders have even used elements of their robust body in their remote-controlled robots.

HIGHEST JUMPER
70cm

This gunk is known as cuckoo spit because it arrives at the same time cuckoos do each year

FROGHOPPER
All around the world

The flea might be the most famous insect jumper, but the froghopper can match its legendary leap... even though it's 60 times heavier! Why do they need to hop so high? Scientists think it's to get from tree to tree without touching the ground. Unlike human high-jumpers, their legs are so well designed for taking off that they can't use them for anything else – froghoppers just drag them along the ground when they're walking. What?!

The legs snap open like a catapult and it's been estimated that their acceleration in the air can be 4,000m per second! Scientists think that the G-force generation from such epic jumps hits the froghopper at up to 80 times more than an astronaut feels blasting into orbit. They also have another name: spittlebugs. The reason the name's so gross is because their nymphs (babies) encase themselves in a foamy bath to stay protected (see above right)! Most bugs feed on sap but the froghopper dilutes it and climbs into the warm, sticky mess to stay safe.

THE FROGHOPPER
LOCKS ITS LEGS
BEHIND ITS BACK! THE FORCE IT TAKES TO BREAK THE LOCK **BLASTS IT** INTO THE AIR!

A CAMERA RUNNING AT **2,000 FRAMES PER SECOND** COULDN'T CATCH THE ACTION

RUNNERS-UP

FLEAS

KATYDIDS

GRASSHOPPER

MEGALOPTERA   WATER STRIDER   WATER BOATMEN

Giant water bugs can tackle prey larger than themselves - fish, ducks, snakes and even turtles

ACTUAL SIZE

GIANT WATER BUG
Venezuela / Brazil

This bright-eyed bug can be found swimming in freshwater habitats worldwide but you might not want to meet one after you've read this! The giant water bug may live in water but their vampire-hunting style lets them suck their prey dry! Sitting just under the surface of ponds, marshes and streams, they take on prey many times their own size, grabbing them with their raptorial (raptor – just like the dinosaur) claws and liquefying their insides with a venomous strain of saliva. Shocking!

Insects don't have lungs – instead, they have tiny holes in their bodies called spiracles that connect to air-filled tubes. Giant water bugs collect oxygen using the tip of their abdomen. That's right: they use their bottom to breathe! They can also capture air bubbles under their wings as they swim, swallowing them to stay underwater even longer. This brutal beastie has been known to take on ducks, snakes and even turtles and win!

LARGEST AQUATIC INSECT
12cm

Wu LD'S CUULEST BUGS ❄️

Any animal must be hardy to survive the freezing cold, and these chilly creepy-crawlies are no different! Cold can be a matter of life and death for insects – these are some of the ultimate survivors

-150°C

BANDED WOOLLY BEAR CATERPILLARS ↓

This caterpillar might look fluffy, but there's more helping it stay alive than just its warm coat! Eventually emerging as the beautiful Isabella tiger moths, banded woolly bear caterpillars produce a chemical called glycerol, which works a lot like antifreeze in a car! As the weather turns colder, this cool chemical stops their inner cells from dying – they can survive temperatures as low as -70°C. Cool!

FACT THE BANDED WOOLLY BEAR CATERPILLAR CAN REPEAT THIS **DEFROSTING PROCESS** MANY TIMES OVER THE SAME WINTER! IF THERE ARE PLANTS AROUND FOR THEM TO EAT, THEIR SUPPLY OF GLYCEROL WON'T RUN OUT.

RED FLAT BARK BEETLE ↑

Most insects use leaves and rocks to burrow beneath, but the red flat bark beetle can even use snow as a blanket! Similar to when we cosy up under a duvet, it works like insulation for this beetle – but how cold can they really get? Scientists have lowered their temperature to a chilly -150°C... and they still didn't freeze! How does this compare to nature? The coldest ever temperature on Earth was -129°C in Antarctica in 1983! Just like upis beetles, they use glycerol to protect their cells and lose lots of water.

FACT SCIENTISTS HAVE BEEN FASCINATED BY THE NATURAL **ANTIFREEZE-LIKE** TECHNIQUES OF THESE BEETLES, AS THEY'LL HOPEFULLY REVOLUTIONISE THE WAY WE CAN **PRESERVE HUMAN ORGANS**, DE-ICE AIRCRAFTS AND EVEN **STORE ICE CREAM!**

-70°C

FUNGUS GNAT ↑

Some insects are thought of as pests by people all over the world, but the fungus gnat has proven it's pretty good at surviving anything we put it through – even the cold! Advice on getting rid of these tiny survivors used to suggest that freezing infested sections of their homes would put an end to gnats, but research suggests they're much hardier than humans thought. Most insects here have adapted to the coldest climates... the fungus gnat is just trying to survive a little closer to home!

LESSER STAG BEETLE LARVAE ↑

As humans, we rely on our parents and guardians to help keep us safe from nasty weather – growing grubs aren't so lucky! Lesser stag beetle larvae need to be built of stronger stuff to survive and in some cases, they can grow up to 11cm long. Unlike the larvae of the bigger stag beetle, these grubs can be found above ground. While most hibernating bugs and insects will stay still, lesser stag beetle larvae respond to predators (even when the temperature's freezing!) to escape.

UPIS BEETLE ↓

Also known as the Alaskan darkling beetle, it might not look like it's ready for the cold, but it can withstand wintry conditions as cold as -100°C! Its insides work overtime and the upis survives thanks to sugar. It's able to produce a sugar-based frost-busting liquid called xylomannan, which lines the membranes of its cells. This really is a last resort though – upis beetles will dig deep into aspen and willow trees to avoid the ice.

FAST FACTS

1. How do most species survive the cold? In the autumn, monarch butterflies migrate thousands of kilometres from America to Mexico, to find warmer climates that aren't so cruel to bugs!

2. Humans haven't got a hope of competing with these icy insects! The coldest a body temperature has dropped to and survived is 13.7°C.

3. Insect hibernation is known as diapause. They enter a state of suspended animation called torpor in loose leaves or under rocks.

TOP 10 DANGEROUS

Not all insects are harmless! From the most painful bites to deadly disease spreaders, these arachnids and insects put the creepy in creepy-crawly. These ten terrors can cause serious damage!

← BLACK WIDOW SPIDER

Packing a nasty bite with a venom 15 times stronger than a rattlesnake, the black widow can be recognised by the scarlet hourglass on its abdomen. The marking's a warning to any creature in the animal kingdom, but as bare-bottomed humans have moved away from old outhouses to toilets indoors to do their business, its threat has dwindled. In fact, the animal most at risk from the black widow's bite is the male black widow! They get their name from their willingness to eat the male of the species!

THREAT LEVEL 6

KILLER BEE →

When two species of insects breed among themselves, the results can be a shockingly treacherous hybrid! When Brazilian scientists imported African honeybees to breed more effective workers, the bees escaped and bred with the local species. It sounds like something from a sci-fi movie, but killer bees will hunt a threat for half a kilometre if provoked! In humans, the stings are still savage – they've led to nausea and even breathing problems.

THREAT LEVEL 7

BUGS

DRIVER ANT →

Found in Central Africa, driver ants have the biggest colonies of any creature on the planet, often numbering up to 22 million. Imagine a wave of insects tearing into anything in its way – they do have stingers, but it's their shockingly strong jaws we should worry about! Indigenous people of the Congo have been known to coax and control driver ants to wipe out whole nests of pests. Even the most dangerous insects on the planet can be weaponised!

THREAT LEVEL
8

← MOSQUITOES

If you're counting casualties, then the mosquito is likely the most dangerous animal in the world! You might not guess because of its size, but that tiny mouth packs a punch. Its proboscis is a complicated system made up of six thin spears – the bite itself isn't all that painful, but that's part of the problem. As bloodsuckers, mosquitoes transmit diseases from one target to the next, including malaria, zika virus and dengue fever, all of which can be deadly!

THREAT LEVEL
10

RED FIRE ANTS →

They're only 1cm long, but the red fire ant is named because its bite is much worse than it should be for a species of its size. Too many bites, and it's game over for most species – the shock of the sting is too much for the central nervous system. Building their colonies underfoot, like most insects, they'll attack when they think you or your toes are a threat. Their colonies are big enough to have multiple queens – if one falls, the colony doesn't!

THREAT LEVEL
7

BRAZILIAN WANDERING SPIDER →

Considered to be the most toxic spider on the planet, the Brazilian wandering spider is a menace on the move! It'll rest in cosy spots out of sight, like fruits and flowers, until it's hungry – which is when it'll start to explore, ready to sink its super-sized fangs into insects and small animals. While it's been known to bite humans, it has what's known as a dry bite, which is what we're likely to get if it's not feeling too threatened.

THREAT LEVEL 6

THREAT LEVEL 7

ASIAN GIANT HORNET →

Hornets of any size are known to be seriously dangerous but the Asian giant hornet's stinger is on another scale of pain – it can be 6mm long! As with most animals, humans aren't giant hornets' first targets, but they're attracted to our odours... if there's sugar and sweat in the air, they'll start the hunt. American scientists have waged war on these huge hornets recently because they've been known to wipe out whole colonies of bees when attacking!

TARANTULA HAWK →

What's scarier than a tarantula? This woeful wasp's way of caring for its young involves attacking a full-size tarantula, paralysing it with its powerful sting and dragging it back to its nest. There, it lays an egg on the back of the spider... you can guess what happens next! It becomes an eight-legged buffet for the next generation of tarantula hawks. It tends to avoid humans, but it's said that its sting will make you scream out loud!

LAYING ITS EGGS IN A TARANTULA!

THREAT LEVEL
8

THREAT LEVEL
7

← KISSING BUG

Keep your mouth shut! Hungry for moisture and carbon dioxide, the kissing bug might have a cute name, but it's also known as the vampire bug – beware of its bite! These mini menaces aim for the mouth while people sleep. Like mosquitoes, these biting bugs carry diseases. Have you heard the myth that spiders fall into your mouth while you sleep? It's not real, but the kissing bug is!

THE ANT-EATING ASSASSIN BUG PILES ITS VICTIMS ON TOP OF ITSELF TO SCARE PREDATORS

ASP CATERPILLAR →

It might look like a coconut husk, but beneath the stunning coat of the asp caterpillar lie venomous spines which stick into a predator's skin. Victims of its venom have reportedly gone into comas due to the pain! Also called the puss moth caterpillar, it's known to cause terrible rashes – because its vile venom is meant for hunters far smaller than humans, the pain thankfully goes within an hour.

THREAT LEVEL
5

LIGHT UP THE NIGHT

When torches aren't available, nature finds a way! Bioluminescence means light and life and it's a seriously smart way of seeing in the dark. These stunning species glow to communicate, mate and even shock predators!

GLITTERING GLOW-WORMS ↓

Also called fungus gnats, the glittering glow-worms of New Zealand are a natural wonder, living deep under the Earth. If you're brave enough to venture down into the Waitomo Caves, you'll find them lining the walls like an underground sea of stars. Secreting sticky, venomous fishing lures to the water beneath them, they creep down the lines to catch their petrified prey.

FACT WAITOMO'S GLOW-WORM IS A GRUB FOR NINE MONTHS AND ONLY SURVIVES AS AN ADULT FOR A FEW DAYS!

FIREFLIES ↑

Ever meet someone and just feel like they're speaking the same language as you? Fireflies do too! Males will fire out a unique pattern of coloured light bursts from their abdomen and if a female flashes in the same style they'll couple up! It's not always as lovely as it sounds, though – some females fake this loving light show and devour males to steal their defensive chemicals!

FACT THE GLOWING ENZYME IN FIREFLIES IS USED IN VARIOUS SCIENTIFIC PROCEDURES TO TRACK THE SPREAD OF INFECTION AND EVEN CONFIRM DISEASES.

GLOWING CLICK BEETLES →

Also known as the headlight elator, the glowing click beetle's high beams are on its head. Adults can switch up the intensity of their light like a dimmer switch and eat everything from fermenting fruit to other grubs to keep the lights on. They can hurl themselves into the air with a snap and can be seen for 50 metres through the trees.

FACT SCIENTISTS THINK THE CLICK BEETLE'S FULL BEAMS WARN PREDATORS, WHILE THEIR STOMACH SHINE IS USED TO MATE.

← RAILROAD WORMS

It's a neat trick to shine a light in the animal kingdom but how about two colours? Railroad worms are named after their track-like markings, which glow. Just like a stop light, their red head is a warning for predators to stay away! They're beautiful without their lights on but scientists think their bright markings are a clear sign to attackers that they'd taste terrible!

FACT THE FEMALE RAILROAD WORM IS WHAT'S KNOWN AS A LARVIFORM SPECIES – IT NEVER GROWS OUT OF ITS BABY FORM.

GLOWING SCORPION

It's not just insects that glow in the dark! Strangely, scorpions glow under the ultraviolet shine of the Moon. Some scientists think it might be to lull enemies into a false sense of security before they get stung! Scorpions have incredible eyesight and being able to reflect the Moon's rays back out into their hunting grounds could be a natural version of night vision.

FACT SCORPIONS' SHIELDING IS SUPER TOUGH AND THE GLOW COMES FROM HYALINE, WHICH IS SIMILAR TO HUMAN CARTILAGE.

OUT OF THIS
WORLD!

We can't believe these arachnids and insects aren't from another planet... or are they?! Here are the weirdest, wildest, most alien-looking arthropods in our universe

SPINY FLOWER MANTIS →

Looking like a piece of living coral reef, this African alien is one of the smaller mantis species, but it's still an incredible hunter! Its knobbly body, intricate spikes and green and white colouration combo lead a lot of insects to believe it's an exotic plant. When they come to pollinate, the spiny flower mantis attacks – murder is on the menu for this mantis!

ALIEN ABILITY The spiny flower mantis can also use its dramatic colours to shock would-be predators. It uses the eyespots on its wings to create a fearsome face – it's called a deimatic display.

← WHIP SPIDER

When is a spider not a spider? The whip spider has evolved to be even greater – two of its eight legs have transformed into extrasensory antenniform! These super sensitive whips make them incredible hunters and they can home in on prey and their nests. Unlike most spiders, Amblypygids (meaning blunt tail) don't possess any silk-making glands or venomous fangs. In fact, the only way they attack enemies is by sinking their thorny arms (called pedipalps) into prey!

ALIEN ABILITY Whip spiders can survive for a month without food, which suits their nervous nature. With no paralysing venom to save them, they prefer to keep themselves to themselves – a fact we're fine with!

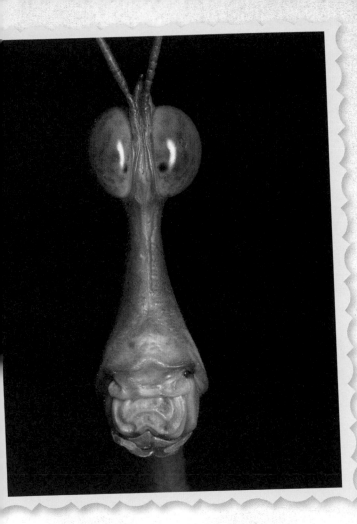

← HORSEHEAD GRASSHOPPER

Why the long face? This odd South American grasshopper looks like a mash-up of a grasshopper and a stick insect! Their tall, gormless faces and bright-green colouring make them look as much like an animated bug as an alien. The females are usually even bigger than the males, but both sexes of the horsehead grasshopper pack super-strong back legs, which help them leap up to 20 times their body length. Just like an astronaut, this horse-headed hopper can defy gravity. It's *A Bug's Life*!

ALIEN ABILITY Horsehead grasshoppers can grow from freshly hatched to adult size in a few short weeks and their early life stages are called instars. All insects grow by shedding their exoskeletons and growing new ones underneath – the removed skeleton (the exuvia) looks just like a hollowed-out horsehead grasshopper!

FACT SOME SPECIES OF TARDIGRADE CAN SURVIVE BONE-CHILLING TEMPERATURES AS COLD AS -272.15°C. WE CAN'T IMAGINE HOW COLD THAT IS!

TARDIGRADE →

Also known as the moss piglet, this minuscule monster might not have come from outer space, but it can certainly survive there! Tardigrades are microscopic, eight-legged animals that aren't exactly insects, but they're related to arthropods (animals like crustaceans and insects which have exoskeletons). Tardigrades can exist just about anywhere, but they prefer to live in damp moss and underwater sediment. Because there's over 1,100 species of them, they've adapted to life in moss, plants and the sea. How do they eat? They suck the life out of cells... and that sounds pretty alien to us!

ALIEN ABILITY Tardigrades are built to survive all sorts of extreme environments! Going into a tun state – sometimes for decades – they can drop their metabolism to 0.01% of its normal rate. When it's safe, they revive themselves. Back from the dead!

GIANT LONG-LEGGED KATYDID →

They may look frightening, but the Macrolyristes corporalis is actually very gentle! Found in Malaysia's mountainous forest, they stay motionless during the day and use their camouflage to confuse their predators. With their green skin and beady black eyes, katydids are one of the most alien-looking insects around, and their extra-long antennae can even outstretch the length of their bodies, growing up to three times longer.

ALIEN ABILITY Male katydids scream a horrible, high-pitched sound to call for females – it's called stridulation. It's suspected that they're one of the loudest insects in existence. Given that they're one of the biggest too, it makes sense. Coupled with their super-sensitive antennae, you'd be wise to expect that they could communicate with life beyond Earth!

← DEVIL'S FLOWER MANTIS

Another Martian-faced mantis, the devil's flower species is known as idolomantis diabolica... diabolic by name and nature! While they're born black to look like ants and deter predators, they grow into walking wood shavings, with bright red, white, blue and black markings lining the inside of their deadly arms. You can't see these colours when the mantis is resting, but when it's time to defend itself, the colours come out in force. Despite its devilish appearance, this mysterious mantis is known to get stressed easily and will run away from danger in a panicked frenzy!

ALIEN ABILITY The devil's flower mantis has its own built-in armour, but it doesn't look like a shield. In fact, it looks like a dried leaf! This is a brilliant example of an insect evolving to blend in with its surroundings – its armour doubles as deep-cover camouflage.

THORN BUG →

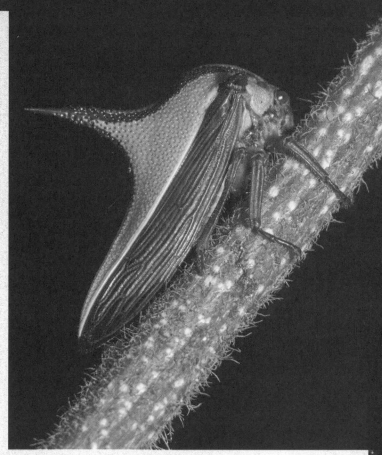

It's an alien infestation! These shiny thorn-shaped insects can suck the life out of trees! Forming dense clusters around plants, they'll overrun forests in Florida and infest their targets until there's nothing left. Why do they do it? Sucking the sap from trees is a smart way to stay well fed. Looking just like the thorns of an alien rosebush, they can hide in plain sight – they're also known as treehoppers, because once these sharp-looking suckers are done, they'll spring off in search of something else to devour.

ALIEN ABILITY The thorn bug is incredibly distasteful! The adults pass a potent chemical down to their nymphs (the name for insects' young). Try to eat it and you'll want to spit it out! Coupled with their spiky shells, it's the perfect method of warding off potential predators.

← SCORPION FLY

With its long beak and scorpion-like tail, this species stalks stinging nettles and brambles, searching for dead insects and stealing the contents of spiders' webs. Yet while it's called the scorpion fly, it doesn't use its tail for stinging, but rather for mating. For lots of male insects, a relationship can mean death – in the scorpion fly's case, it might get eaten! So, it gives its partner a gift: a dead insect or a mass of gooey spit. Not quite a box of chocolates, is it?

ALIEN ABILITY Insects started to fly 350 million years ago – before birds, and even before the dinosaurs! The scorpion fly's baffling design has clearly worked, because scientists think it could have been around for up to 250 million years. If it ain't broke, don't fix it.

CHAPTER 3

BUGS AND US

Some insects, such as crop-eating locusts or disease-spreading mosquitoes, are thought of as pests. Others, such as honeybees or migrating butterflies, are valuable to our ecosystem. Let's take a look at how science is working to prevent pests and using insects' amazing properties to develop medicines and other products...

PESKY PESTS

Bugs are an essential part of the planet's incredible ecosystems (areas where plants, animals and other living organisms work together) but they can be both helpful and harmful

BAD NEWS BUGS

Unfortunately insects can be a real nuisance. Each year, insects destroy 20% of the world's food supply and many transmit diseases to humans, animals and plants. Bugs, such as fleas, tsetse flies and wasps, also cause a lot of discomfort – biting and stinging humans and animals.

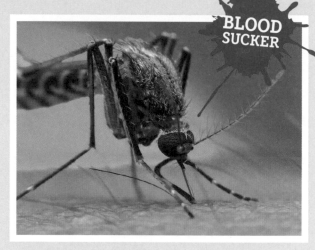

BLOOD SUCKER

▲ Known for their itchy bites, mosquitoes are small, bloodsucking flies. They use six thin, needle-like mouthparts (called stylets) to bite their victim's skin so they can feed on them. Unfortunately mosquitoes can spread serious diseases including malaria, yellow fever, zika and encephalitis

ABSOLUTE STINKER

BLOOD SUCKER

▲ Shield beetles release a smelly pong to protect themselves and are a big threat to crops, eating fruit by sucking out the juice. They really are stink bugs!

▲ Bloodsucking fleas can attack livestock on farms and cause infections in horses, cattle, sheep and pigs. In the 1600s, their diseases wiped out 20% of people in London

PEST WATCH!

Find out why these insects are always unwelcome visitors...

1 Bedbugs

These insects have infested homes for thousands of years. They live in wood and fabric and sneak out at night to feed. They're bloodsuckers and pierce people's skin with their long beak, leaving a small, sore, itchy wound.

2 Termites

Known as 'silent destroyers,' termites destroy wooden structures by eating their way through them. These insects can chew through wood and floors undetected – leaving just a thin layer of paint!

3 Cockroaches

These creepy-crawlies are a common pest in many homes all over the world. Cockroaches come out at night to search for food and communicate by releasing a smelly scent. These insects feed on everything from food and skin to books, shoes and even poo and can spread germs that cause nasty diseases.

BUG☑ MUNCHER

IMPORTANT HELP

Thankfully, the world's insects also do a lot of good! Insects pollinate plants and crops, keep soil healthy, decompose dead plants and animals and are a source of food – for instance, birds eat up to 550 million tons of bugs each year! Plus wasps and ladybirds help protect plants by destroying the caterpillars and aphids that attack them.

Ladybirds munch up to 60 aphids a day and help control garden pests!

APHID☑ CRUNCHER

BUG CONTROL

From vaccines and mosquito nets to pesticides and bug repellent, we've come up with lots of different ways to protect ourselves from insects and the damage they can do

Amazing medicine

Some bug-borne diseases can lead to serious, life-threatening illnesses. Many diseases are spread by insects, such as mosquitoes, fleas and ticks. However, vaccines (medicine that prevents disease) have been created to tackle some of the illnesses – including malaria, trench fever and Lyme disease – and new treatments are being discovered all the time.

FACT THE MOST COMMON WAY TO AVOID MOSQUITO BITES AND PREVENT MALARIA INFECTION IS TO SLEEP UNDER A BED NET THAT'S BEEN TREATED WITH INSECTICIDES (CHEMICALS THAT KILL INSECTS).

BUZZ OFF!

Spray it again!

Insect repellent, also known as bug spray, is often used to ward off insects. It's thought to work by affecting an insect's sense of smell and taste and comes in lots of different forms – including a spray or cream, scented candles and treated wristbands. People have been using insect repellent for thousands of years. Ancient Egyptians burned lamps filled with castor oil to keep pesky bugs away.

PEST ZONE

Unfortunately, insects are responsible for destroying crops around the world. The most common way insects damage crops is by feeding on them but they also harm them indirectly by spreading different types of plant diseases.

All farmers work to prevent pests from ruining the crops they grow and usually deal with insect attacks by spraying crops with insecticides. However, these chemicals can be expensive and harm the environment. Plus, insects are developing resistance to them.

SPECIAL SOLUTIONS

Synthetic pesticides can be bad news for the environment, causing pollution and contamination. So scientists are always looking for new eco-friendly alternatives...

✳ It's thought as much as 98% of pesticides that are sprayed on crops bounce straight off. So a new water-based pesticide that's better at sticking to leaves has been developed.

✳ A natural chemical found in fruit is being tested as a way of protecting fruit from flies.

✳ Bees are being used to distribute a naturally occurring fungus called Clonostachys rosea that helps protect blueberries, strawberries, tomatoes, almonds and sunflowers from disease.

✳ Many insects don't like the strong-smelling desert plant lavender cotton. So some farmers have started using a natural extract from it to keep insect pests away from crops.

FAST⚡FACT

Farmers in Nepal, South Asia, spray their crops with garlic, spices, water and cow urine. The organic liquid pesticide, called Jhol Mol, keeps insects away and protects plants from disease.

BUG POWER

For thousands of years, insects have inspired us to interact with the world for the better. Let's break down the most incredible ways they have changed the world around us

Clean and healthy

Insects and the chemicals extracted from them have been used for thousands of years to help humans. Using insects in medicine is called entomotherapy, and it's likely you know someone who has had a little help from an insect. Around the world, at least 1,000 species of insect are used in medicine!

Blister beetles secrete a substance that helps treat burns

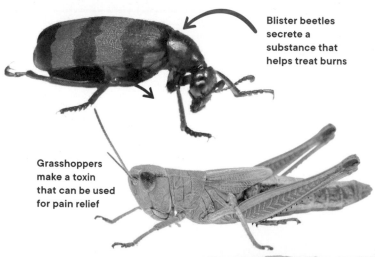

Grasshoppers make a toxin that can be used for pain relief

Bee venom could one day cure rheumatoid arthritis, gout and even multiple sclerosis thanks to its enzymes

Positive produce

Lots of products we use every day simply wouldn't be possible without our insect friends. Cochineal dye, which makes foods red, has been used in everything from wine to sweets. Shellac, which is used in false nails and wood lacquers is a product of the lac scale, while dead darkling beetle armour is the key to making brilliantly biodegradable plastics! The most famous product is definitely honey, though – we've been eating bees' delicious golden gift for millennia. It's even used in medicine!

▶ Cochineal insects are dried and crushed to make a food dye called carmine

◀ Shellac's an ingredient in a wide range of products, from hair sprays to cake glaze

Keeping pests in order

Insects are great at keeping other insects in check! When pests are threatening crops, farmers send in the predators and parasites of the bug world to sort them out! If a harmful weed is spreading, insects can be used to stop the growth (when humans are keeping an eye on them). Ladybirds love to gobble up pesky gnats, while parasites such as lice can spell disaster for dangerous bugs.

Spreading pollen

Over 75% of all flowering plants – including most crops grown by humans – need animals to pollinate them. Countless insects play their part in plant pollination, from bees and beetles to butterflies and moths. Human interference has caused a drop in this vital process, but important groups are working hard to help insects out, introducing new plants into the chain and using less harmful (and more natural) insecticides.

POLLINATION

Edible insects

Insects have been on the menu around the world for longer than you might think! Pliny, the brilliant Roman scholar from the first century, wrote that ancient Romans would often scoff down beetle grubs reared on the finest ingredients. In some societies, entomophagy (the act of eating insects) often appears when other food sources are hard to find. There are more than 1,400 edible species of insects, with the most popular being crickets and mealworms.

What's more, insects could be the key to sustainable snacking! More people in the western world are discovering how bad eating meat is for the planet, and scientists are using insects as ingredients to lessen the effects on our Earth, so tuck in!

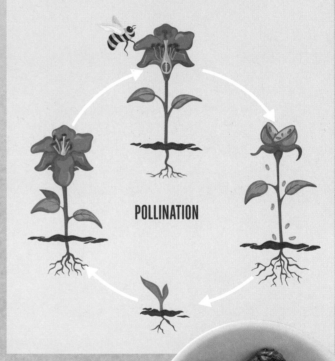

BUILD YOUR OWN
BUG HOTEL

Creepy-crawlies aren't always that cute, so not everyone wants to share their house with them. But most bugs aren't bad guys – in fact, they're good at helping out in the garden. Get insects to stick around by giving them a place where they're always welcome!

What you'll need:
Tools Scissors
Materials 1 x recycled plastic bottle, 1 x pen,
1 x length of string or garden twine approx 60cm,
1 x small twig (about 1cm in diameter and 5cm long),
sticks, twigs, seed heads, pine cones, wood shavings
and lichen

BUILDING YOUR HOTEL

① With the help of an adult, cut the top and the bottom off the plastic bottle with scissors so that you are left with a tube shape.

② Carefully pierce a hole in the middle of the tube, using a pen or scissors, and another hole underneath on the opposite side.

③ Thread the length of string through both holes. Pull it through, leaving a tail of about 7.5cm. Tie this tail around the small twig to prevent it pulling out of the hole. Leave enough string at the opposite end to be able to tie a loop to hang the bug hotel up.

④ Gather up some natural materials for filling the plastic tube: sticks, twigs, moss, pine cones, dried leaves etc. Your insect friends will love this!

⑤ Fill the bottle with the bug-friendly materials you have collected. Make sure everything is tightly packed together with tiny crevices for your bugs to hide in. Hang it up in your garden using the loop of string and wait for the beasties to find their way in. The more, the merrier!

What's the bug idea?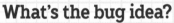

Insects make up more than half of all living things, with 1.4 billion insects for every person on the planet. That's a lot of bugs needing a place to stay! They can live anywhere, from the snowiest mountain to the hottest desert, but why not look out for the ones found in your own backyard?

Most bugs are good guys! They clean up and add goodness to the soil to help food grow. Some pollinate flowers to grow delicious fruits, while others fight the bad bugs who munch their way through any fruit, vegetables or plants growing in the garden. They might not be as cuddly as pets, but they're handy to have around!

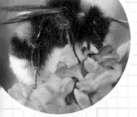

FIVE STEPS TO AN
INSECT-FRIENDLY GARDEN

You can't call them in or leave food out but there are a few bright ways to bring all the best bugs to your backyard

1 Flower power

Planting flowers that bugs go for the most is the easiest way to keep them sweet. Start by scattering a packet of wildflower seeds – ladybirds love these, as do pollinators such as butterflies and bees. Flying insects like bright colours, but pollinators in particular are drawn to blooms with a strong fragrance because they use their sense of smell, not sight, to find food plants. Heady-smelling lavender in the summer, for example, is rich in nectar.

As well as smells, different shapes of flower will draw different insects in. The long, thin tubes of honeysuckle are popular with butterflies, while bellflowers, clover and foxgloves are best for bees. Both like flat flowers such as ox-eye daisies, marigolds and wild yarrow – as do hoverflies, who are super-helpful to have around. Just one of their larvae will devour 400 sap-sucking aphids!

2 Let it grow

Most people don't want a garden that looks messy or overgrown, but it's good to let a little corner or two go wild! Not every patch of lawn needs mowing – longer grass gives insects like skipper butterflies some shelter, where they can lay their eggs. It also allows wild yarrow to flower in between the blades, bringing in more bees.

People tend to cut them back, but even weeds have a part to play. Dandelions are an excellent source of nectar for insects and some caterpillars will only feed on nettles, thistles and ragwort, so keep a spot aside for them. Nobody likes getting stung, so perhaps plant nettles in a pot to stop them spreading. Go wild, but not too wild!

3 Log out

More fun to make than a compost heap, log piles are easy to build and look after. Find a damp spot that's not too dark but not too sunny, pile the biggest logs on the bottom and layer with loose twigs and leaves to build a pyramid. Larger logs with bark still attached work best. Keep it watered during dry spells and you can expect woodlice, spiders, ground beetles, millipedes and centipedes, earwigs and even overwintering bumblebees to move in! If you don't have room for a log pile, leave a few leaves lying around in winter. This creates a safe space for even the smallest critters to hide until spring.

4 It's a bug-bath!

Ponds with lily pads to land on are perfect for all kinds of wildlife, but not everyone has one or can dig one. Try building a bug-bath instead! As with a bird-bath, fill a shallow container with gravel and just enough water to keep it moist. You could even use an upturned dustbin lid and let it fill with rainwater, which bees like best. Litter it with some larger stones, so insects can rest and can drink water without falling in and drowning. Try adding a few floating corks to give them somewhere to land!

5 Try not to use pesticides

Finally, don't spray insect-killing stuff around the garden! Pesticides are agents that poison the insects we consider pests but they harm the helpful ones too.

WHAT TO DO WITH A WINDOW BOX

If you don't have a garden, you can still woo butterflies and bees to your window or balcony with a brightly coloured window box.

Choose plants with simple flowers that are attractive to insects and provide pollen and nectar. Make sure the box is lined with plastic, has holes for water to drain, then layer it with plants that will flower one after another from February to summer.

Start with crocuses and snowdrops, then daffodils and tulips, then long-lasting wallflowers that will continue to lure pollinators in. Push nasturtium seeds into the compost to keep a bit of bright orange going right into autumn.

Spruce things up by dead-heading (getting rid of old, dry flowers) regularly and you're set for a buzzing success.

THE BIG
BUG QUIZ

Read the book, then put your newfound knowledge to the test!

1. What insect has ears on its knees? (*Turn to page 9 for a hint*)

2. What are exoskeletons made of? (*Turn to page 10 for a hint*)

3. How many sections do insect bodies have? (*Turn to page 10 for a hint*)

4. What is insect poo called? (*Turn to page 12 for a hint*)

5. How many stages are there in the lifecycle of a cockroach? (*Turn to page 15 for a hint*)

6. What beetle is strong enough to survive being run over by a car? (*Turn to page 23 for a hint*)

7. What part of its body does the bombardier beetle spray chemicals out of? (*Turn to page 24 for a hint*)

8. How high was the tallest ever termite mound? (*Turn to page 28 for a hint*)

9. Where did the Hallucigenia sparsa have teeth? (*Turn to page 35 for a hint*)

10. What special food are queen bees fed? (*Turn to page 36 for a hint*)

11. What colour is the 22-spot ladybird? (*Turn to page 43 for a hint*)

12. What is a brood ball? (*Turn to page 44 for a hint*)

13. How many wings does a butterfly have? (*Turn to page 47 for a hint*)

14 What are dragonflies' extra eyes called? (*Turn to page 49 for a hint*)

15 What is the world's heaviest spider? (*Turn to page 51 for a hint*)

16 Which species of tarantula can float down to the forest floor? (*Turn to page 55 for a hint*)

17 What is the name of the deadly scorpion mating dance? (*Turn to page 57 for a hint*)

18 How loud was the world's loudest cicada? (*Turn to page 63 for a hint*)

19 How far do globe skimmers migrate? (*Turn to page 65 for a hint*)

20 Which crazy creature has extrasensory antenniform? (*Turn to page 76 for a hint*)

21 What substance is it that makes scorpions glow in moonlight? (*Turn to page 75 for a hint*)

22 How many aphids can a ladybird munch in a day? (*Turn to page 83 for a hint*)

23 What is Jhol Mol? (*Turn to page 85 for a hint*)

24 What substance could one day be used to treat rheumatoid arthritis? (*Turn to page 86 for a hint*)

25 What is entomophagy? (*Turn to page 87 for a hint*)

93

GLOSSARY

ABDOMEN
The end part of an insect's body, where important organs are stored.

ANTENNAE
Long sensory organs on the heads of insects that they use to navigate their environment.

ARTHROPOD
Animals without backbones, but with exoskeletons, segmented bodies and jointed limbs.

BIODEGRADABLE
Something that can be broken down by bacteria or other living things and will not contribute to pollution.

COLONY
A community of insects of the same kind living in a shared structure.

CONTINENT
One of the world's seven large continuous regions of land.

DIAPAUSE
When an insect enters a period of suspended animation to save energy and survive dangerous weather conditions.

ELYTRA
The hard wing cases that some species of insects have.

ENTOMOLOGIST
A scientist who studies insects.

EXOSKELETON
A hard outer skeleton that protects an insect's body.

FRASS
Insect poo.

HYDRAULIC
Movement or action brought about by pressurised fluids.

INVERTEBRATES
A group of animals that have no spine.

LARVA
The infant form of any species of insect that will transform greatly once it develops into an adult.

MEMBRANE
A thin layer of tissue or cells in an insect's or animal's body.

METABOLISM
The chemical reactions that take place inside an animal's body to produce necessary energy.

METAMORPHOSIS
When something, like an insect, changes from one form to another.

MIMIC
When something pretends to be something else.

MOULTING
When an insect sheds an old layer of skin from its body.

NYMPH
The young form of any type of insect that does not change much physically as it grows into an adult.

PINCERS
Sharp organs used by some insects to attack and tear apart prey or defend themselves from attack.

POLLINATION
The transfer of pollen by insects, other animals or the wind, allowing plants to be fertilised and reproduce.

PROBOSCIS
A straw-like tube through which some insects feed.

PUPA
Also known as a chrysalis. The stage between larva and adult when the insect is undergoing a major physical transformation.

THORAX
The middle part of an insect's body to which the legs are attached.

TOXIC
Something that is poisonous or harmful to a living thing.

URTICATING
Something that gives an irritating or stinging sensation.

VENOM
A poisonous substance produced by some insects that it uses to kill prey or defend itself from predators.

VIVIPARITY
When an egg develops inside the body of the parent animal.

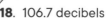

QUIZ ANSWERS

1. Grasshopper
2. Chitin
3. Three
4. Frass
5. Three
6. The diabolical ironclad beetle
7. Its bum!
8. 12.8 metres
9. In its throat!
10. Royal jelly
11. Yellow
12. A poo ball covered in dung beetle eggs
13. Four
14. Ocelli
15. Goliath tarantula
16. Gooty sapphire tarantula
17. Promenade à deux
18. 106.7 decibels
19. 6,000km
20. Whip spider
21. Hyaline
22. Up to 60
23. An organic liquid pesticide
24. Bee venom
25. The act of eating insects

INDEX

First published 2023 by Button Books, an imprint of Guild of Master Craftsman Publications Ltd, Castle Place, 166 High Street, Lewes, East Sussex, BN7 1XU, UK. Copyright in the Work © GMC Publications Ltd, 2023. ISBN 978 1 78708 132 1. Distributed by Publishers Group West in the United States. All rights reserved. No part of this publication may be reproduced, stored in a retrieval system, or transmitted in any form or by any means without the prior permission of the publisher and copyright owner. While every effort has been made to obtain permission from the copyright holders for all material used in this book, the publishers will be pleased to hear from anyone who has not been appropriately acknowledged and to make the correction in future reprints. The publishers and authors can accept no legal responsibility for any consequences arising from the application of information, advice, or instructions given in this publication.
A catalogue record for this book is available from the British Library. Editorial: Susie Duff, Nick Pierce, Lauren Jarvis, Sam Taylor, Vincent Vincent, Rachel Roberts. Design: Jo Chapman, Tim Lambert. Publisher: Jonathan Grogan. Production: Jim Bulley. Photos/illustrations: Shutterstock.com, Science Photo Library, Depositphotos, Michelle Urra, Lou Baker Smith. With special thanks to Ashley Bradford. Colour origination by GMC Reprographics. Printed and bound in China.